# LIGHTER
## LIVING TANTRA

Prana Regina Barrett

Cover and graphic design by Iain Barrett-Byrnes, 3D artist and designer

Photography by Tera Cooley, Freelance Beauty Service LLC
and Benjamin Buren, AliveStudios.com

All rights reserved. No part of this book may be reproduced or utilized in any form or by any means, electronic or mechanical, including photocopying, recording, or by any information storage and retrieval system, without permission in writing from the publisher/author.

Note to readers: This book is intended as an informational guide. The approaches and techniques described within are meant to supplement and not be a substitute for professional medical care or treatment. They should not be used to treat a serious ailment without prior consultation with a qualified health care professional.

Copyright © 2014 Evolve Press
All rights reserved.

ISBN-10  1494361035
ISBN-13  9781494361037

Library of Congress Control Number: 2013922450
CreateSpace Independent Publishing Platform
North Charleston, South Carolina

# Foreward

The philosophy of Tantra to Love™ came to me while doing a fire purification ceremony. I symbolically tossed into the fire what was not serving me, expressed deep gratitude for all the blessings in my life, sat in meditation and called in support in assisting my community. I live in a community where addiction is a common theme. I had endured my share of suffering being around it and attempting to offer support. I feel a strong level of compassion for those who feel trapped in addiction. It was so present in my life that I felt a strong call to ask for guidance.

In my meditation, I saw a grid of light connecting Sky and Earth. The diamond-shaped grid crossed and created a diamond body within my center. The base of its upper point came from the Earth and ended at my heart center. The base of its lower point began in the Sky and ended at my root center. I was then sent a clear message that what is required is to balance Earth and Sky energy and seal that energy in one's center. This translated to me as a combination of *Tantra* yoga and *Qigong* practices that are now the foundation of all Tantra to Love™ programs. This balancing of Sky and Earth energy, while strengthening one's true identity, was clearly a healing practice for more than just those overcoming addiction, but for all choosing to transform.

An intentional Tantra yoga and Qigong lifestyle, guided by an experienced master-level Tantra educator, can balance *Shiva*/masculine/*yang*/

Sky energy and *Shakti*/feminine/*yin*/Earth energy and seal this new way of being in one's center.

In the system of yoga, masculine energy, called Shiva, is drawn from the sky and can be very energizing. In Traditional Chinese Medicine, this is called *yang* energy. Feminine energy is drawn from the Earth and is called Shakti in yoga and *yin* in Traditional Chinese Medicine.

I feel yoga and Qigong should be practiced separately, rather than blending them, because they are different systems and different traditions. I have found that yoga can be very energizing, except for restorative yoga, and this is why I began to practice Qigong, as a way to ground *kundalini* energy. When I practice, I do Qigong first, then yoga. They are both beneficial to supporting Tantra and sacred sexuality practices.

The word Tantra is very misunderstood. I studied Tantra yoga for many years and until I sought it out, it did not include sacred sexuality practices. How we define Tantra at Tantra to Love™ is that it is a lifestyle practice that includes movement, meditation, sound, breath and bodywork. When Tantra is practiced regularly, one's energy centers, also known as *chakras*, begin to open and one begins to expand into one's true nature. Tantric practices increase sensation, enhancing all life experiences, including one's connection with and awareness of oneself and others. Sexuality is a part of life, and thus is included in tantric lifestyle practices, but is only one aspect of Tantra. Today, a new term has been created for Tantra that focuses primarily on sexuality practices: "neotantra."

Qigong is a practice of aligning breath, movement and awareness for exercise, healing and meditation. With roots in Traditional Chinese Medicine, martial arts and Taoist philosophy, Qigong is traditionally viewed as a practice to cultivate and balance *qi* (chi) or life energy. From a philosophical perspective, Qigong is believed to help develop human potential, allow access to higher realms of awareness, and awaken one's "true nature."

*Lighter: Living Tantra* guides the reader to create the balance of Earth and Sky energies within their life, while practicing Tantra and living a tantric lifestyle. The book provides support for opening chakras, for transforming the emotions that emerge, and for the expansion that happens as one opens more fully into one's True Self.

# Acknowledgements

Derek Edry and Laura Webb for their interest in the project and contribution as proofreaders.

Amanda Painter for taking the book to its final publication stage through expert editing and a sincere interest in the topic.

Tera Cooley, of Freelance Beauty Service LLC, for her generous and professional photo shoot.

I thank my husband John Rene Berard for his unconditional support, proof reading, home-cooked meals and extra help around the house while I brought the book to its final publication stage.

Michael Lee for creating Phoenix Rising Yoga Therapy and for his contributions to the blog and book.

Sylvia Brallier for her long term mentoring and contributions to the blog and book.

Ann Carroll, Ph.D., for sharing Qigong, Traditional Chinese Medicine and Taoist philosophy so authentically. I also thank her for opening her home to photo shoots and for her contribution to the blog and book.

Iain Barrett-Byrnes for his 3D design contribution to the book cover and illustrations, his open mind and his willingness to learn a little bit about what his Mom does for a living.

Bethany Mateosian for her contribution to the book and generous Master Level classical Pilates instruction.

All our friends and devoted students for financially supporting the publication of this book.

Robyn Vogel for being my Tantra ally and supporter with unconditional love and friendship.

A special thanks to Martha Williams for noticing my potential and supporting me like a sister along the Tantra educator and author journey. She is my Earth angel.

Sayta Gita Van Dyke, Sylvia Brallier, Karen HassKarl, Micheal Lee, BabaJi, Swami VajraMa and the greater Eldorado Ashram Sangah, The Ram Das Kundalini Yoga Ashram, The Church of Heart Consciousness, The Standing Wave Community, Sandra Boston, Steve and Lokita Carter, Yang Yang, Ph.D., and Ann Carroll, Ph.D., for having such a profound influence on what I share with others today.

I am grateful to my parents Paul Barrett and Milly Curtin for providing a home environment that allowed for open sexuality and body awareness.

# Contents

## Chapter 1: Why Choose a Tantric Lifestyle? — 1
*Defines Tantra, the history of Tantra in the U.S. and how Tantra practices open the physical and emotional body to transformation and living one's true calling. The Third Eye Meditation is offered in this chapter for those who are just beginning to explore Tantra. It is a simple practice that promotes* kundalini *energy activation, inviting the energy centers in the body to open and expand over time.*

## Chapter 2: Self Love — 13
*Guides readers to begin taking care of their body and mind, so they can gently expand and transform. This chapter includes helpful lifestyle suggestions that can be applied easily in daily life, and introductory Qigong and tantric yoga practices.*

## Chapter 3: Transforming Ego — 31
*Transforming ego is the main premise behind the science and methodology of traditional tantric practices. When one is willing to surrender and be vulnerable, one can then expand into one's true identity.*

## Chapter 4: Clear, Honest and Loving Communication — 37
*Guides the reader to learn to communicate in new ways, so they can live the life they are meant to live with ease and harmony.*

## Chapter 5: Community, Companionship and Partnership — 41
*Helps the Tantra practitioner to understand that life is a solo journey, but also how to access support and how to maintain one's uniqueness in relationship with others.*

## Chapter 6: The Shadow and How It Plays into Getting Along with Others     47

*Defines the shadow side of our personality, how to notice it and learn from it. The shadow side of the personality is what seems to cause us to struggle in life. With awareness of the shadow, one can learn to transform this aspect of Self to a lighter way of being in the world, while experiencing more peace and self-acceptance.*

## Chapter 7: Maintaining Your Center and Integrating     51

*Once the reader begins to expand into their true purpose, as a result of applying the practices in the book, this chapter provides guidance for solidifying these changes in the body, mind and spirit.*

## Chapter 8: Sharing Energy     75

*Reinforces the need for a solo practice, while introducing the factors that come into play when sharing energy in partner practices. This chapter provides detailed instructions for eye gazing, hugging, synchronized and circular breathing exercises, as well as ways to ground and center oneself when sharing energy with a partner.*

## Chapter 9: Some Final Thoughts     91

## Appendix: Divine Love Meditation     93

## Glossary of Sanskrit and Chinese Terms     95

## Citations     99

## Recommended Resources     101

*On my way home from my Qigong lesson,
I parked my car and began walking toward my house.
I saw a man in his mid-30s walking toward me holding a black-eyed Susan.
He looked at the flower, spinning it in his hand.
He looked at me and pushed the flower through the air toward me and said,
"This is for you." I smiled, took the flower and thanked him.
He continued on his way. There was no flirtation between us:
just pure love and gratitude. His act of kindness came from
a pure, childlike place in his heart. He made my day. This is Tantra.*

~ *Prana Regina Barrett*

CHAPTER ONE

# Why Choose a Tantric Lifestyle?

Since the late 1980s and into the '90s, when American sex educators such as Annie Sprinkle and Margot Anand invited us to expand our awareness of sexuality, a new and explosive interest in Tantra has begun to surface. After a collective period of separation and individuation, there now appears to be a cultural longing for more connection and intimacy in relationships. As people become more enlightened as a whole, heavily influenced by the yoga revolution, there is also a call, more specifically, for sacred and spiritual connections. People of all ages, genders and sexual orientations are feeling the need for a place to connect with their body, mind and spirit in community.

For those who are new to Tantra, it is a practice that combines movement, breath, meditation and sound to assist the energy system within the body, also known as *chakras*, to open. This opening allows dormant energy, also known as kundalini, to move up from the pelvis, along the spine. As this life-force energy moves up the spine, it helps one to transform and heal. The healing involves loosening constrictions within the body that develop throughout life. When the constrictions are loosened, one's true identity is revealed. When one feels safe to be oneself, one is happier and attracts easily. The expansion of the energy body also increases sensation, clairvoyance and one's ability to connect with others.

Many are sampling Tantra in two-hour or half-day workshops. Those wanting a deeper learning experience attend extended retreats. What I have learned on my own tantric yoga path, and as a Phoenix Rising Yoga Therapist, is that these experiences alone are not enough to open the chakra system and free the kundalini energy. Opening the body to receive the kundalini energy requires transforming a lifetime of parental and societal messages that have caused contraction and holding within the body. This contraction and holding occurs when one is not living one's truth. The body, mind and spirit integrate these openings in the chakra system at a pace that is dependent on physical and emotional history, and is unique for each individual. The body, mind and spirit can only assimilate so much change at once. Consequently, a brief experience will provide a step in the right direction, but will not provide the purification necessary to run kundalini energy and have the Tantra experience you may be seeking.

Attending workshops and retreats is an important first step toward exploring Tantra. One way to deepen the experience is to develop a tantric lifestyle practice with a master teacher; a practice that slowly allows one's chakras to open and expand. In doing so, the practitioner can discover his or her true essence, while fully supported and experiencing the gifts of Tantra. This is a gentle approach, allowing the body, mind and spirit to integrate the chakra openings. Transformation takes place, as well as life shifts: significant physical and emotional health improvements, new jobs, new or deeper partnerships, moves to one's dream location; these are just some of the outcomes I have witnessed.

After studying traditional Tantra yoga for many years with different yoga masters of Kundalini, *Kashmir Shaivism, Standing Wave* and *Ipsalu Kriya,* the kundalini energy began to awaken and I became curious about sacred sexuality. I wanted to learn more about the energy I was feeling and the experience I was having with the kundalini, as it invited my chakras to open and my energy field to expand.

I began to study privately with Tantra teachers who focused more on sacred sexuality and deeper tantric practices. They helped me to understand how to move the energy and use it for personal healing and to enhance my sexual experiences.

My study of Phoenix Rising Yoga Therapy expanded my awareness of chakras. Over the years, I have developed the ability to support individuals when chakras open and emotions are released.

The intention of tantric practices is to expand one's body and experience back to the soul's original essence (known as *purusha* in Sanskrit): who you were as a fetus, free of stress or trauma; and who you are growing into as you become free. This is when we can come into our fullest potential, with acute awareness and clear, loving connection with others.

Chakras can be opened using many modalities, including ecstatic dance, breath work, Qigong, Network Chiropractic, bodywork and yoga, just to mention a few. A combination of Tantra yoga, Qigong, bodywork and emotional healing is the path we share in Tantra to Love™. Our programs are designed to be gentle and healing so participants feel safe and supported as they transform into a new way of being in the world.

On my own Tantra path, and as a practitioner, I have held space for many to expand into their fullest selves. Over and over, I have seen that when chakras open, emotions stir. After all, they became blocked or contracted because one was not protected or did not feel safe being oneself. Contractions can result not only from an accident or abuse, but also from the constant messages we receive from society to be someone we are not. Contractions within the body are a natural response to protect your soul, which wants so much to be free to express itself. However, as you may have gathered in your own life experiences, if we live our lives in fear and are always protecting ourselves, we tend not to be all that successful in life. The contractions affect our ability to create and to let go of unsupportive habits, and also how we connect with others.

A good example is when we go on retreat or vacation and come back happy and inspired. When we relax, soften and open, an internal change can happen. We may feel inspired to write a book, begin a creative project, or have the confidence and joy to make a supportive new friend or meet a future partner.

We can experience this contraction again when we return from vacation and life gets too full and we've allowed ourselves to be pulled off balance. That yummy retreat or vacation feeling is gone and we are back to a contracted state. Sometimes we do manage to tap into the body memory and support that opening, remaining a bit more open than before. In future chapters, I will provide many ways you can support yourself when expanded.

Inviting the chakra system to open requires courage and readiness. If you are not ready, you may not want to take the risk of allowing yourself to be vulnerable. Ready to take that leap, trusting that you will be supported and protected as you heal and open to living your true destiny.

My intention is to provide some insight into how you can feel supported to heal, grow and transform into your fullest potential: your *ananda*; your bliss.

Creating a solid, supportive foundation is the best way to begin this journey. Clear the clutter from your life. Complete unfinished business: both physically, like back taxes due; and emotionally, like making amends with others. It means doing your best to be the best person you can be. Be honest. Make a conscious effort to avoid gossip and to communicate clearly and lovingly, even if it means you need to stick your neck out and be vulnerable. It means being vulnerable — and trusting that when we do our healing with honesty and pure intention, we will be supported.

This has been a big lesson for me, coming from a childhood where I did not feel at all supported by my primary female figure, my mother. I also did not have a strong father figure to protect me. So what did I do in response? I became super-independent at a very early age; I became tough and resourceful, an over-achiever. This behavior causes contractions in the body and in my case, dis-ease (fibromyalgia and breast cancer). It took a lot for me to be able to receive and rely on others, and even more to rely on Spirit, the unseen, to support me fully.

This support sometimes comes in the form of harsh life lessons. When we take the time to listen, heal and grow, abundance, in all its forms, is sure to follow. When we are closer to who we truly are, we are happier. Happy people attract. It's as simple as that.

So now, when times get tough, I just hand it over to The Divine Mother, God, my angels, ancestors and guides. In my meditations, I literally feel myself lying back to allow them to catch me. I let go that much. I completely surrender to perfect and divine timing, trusting that a divine pace is a healthier pace than the U.S. pace / global market pace.

If chakras open too quickly, one can contract around the opening due to fear of being hurt. This is why kundalini activation needs to be a gentle process that happens over time. It's not something that will likely happen in a two-hour or weekend workshop, unless you are already doing a deep, daily chakra-opening practice, like those mentioned above.

Surely there are exceptions: people who had a trauma-free birth and life, and are already running the kundalini energy but don't even know it, or children who were protected but also allowed a level of freedom and creativity their entire childhood. They have always felt safe and free. But even these children can experience contractions because they are so open. These children learn to protect themselves from the not-so-nice people out there, while remaining open and free. A solid foundation helps them to adapt easily to a diverse cultural experience.

In this book, I will cover how to open the chakras slowly and how to take care of yourself as you integrate the openings. The practice I offer is gentle. I move slowly, encouraging deep breath and sound.

I will also share how to ground and create your own bubble of loving protection around you as you expand into your pure essence.

This book is about the healing process that takes place as one lives a tantric lifestyle and experiences all the gifts that lifestyle provides.

Below is a testimonial from one of our clients:

> *"Prana has an exceptional gift to heal others through the use of Phoenix Rising Yoga Therapy (PRYT). She has the unique ability to transform mental constructs and remove negative energies that lodge themselves in one's physical body. Prana's expertise in tantric practices and PRYT has helped me to greater integrate mind,*

*body, soul and spirit toward greater wholeness. Prana has helped me to heal old wounds from childhood trauma, practice forgiveness and compassion toward my sister, achieve greater intimacy with my husband, and gift me with the freedom to accept myself. Namaste Prana!!!"*

*~ Lynn Hendsbee, LCPC-C,*
*Supervisor of Case Managers,*
*Bread of Life Ministries*

But first, we must begin by creating a solid foundation for your journey along your path to expansion, abundance, community and bliss. The following is a simple meditation to help you get started.

### Third Eye Meditation (also known as Spinal Meditation in Ipsalu Kriya Yoga)

This meditation technique opens the crown and third eye chakras (see chakra diagram on page 15) to receive divine energy. It also activates a circuit of energy up and down the spine, opening awareness to the heavens, while maintaining a connection to the Earth.

According to mentor, Sylvia Brallier, this *kriya* "stills the mind, awakens spinal chi, brings the Shiva energy into the body on the inhale and awakens the Shakti energy on the exhale."

Come into a comfortable seated position. Feel your sits bones at the base of your pelvis touching the cushion below you. Feel the backs of your legs touching the cushion and floor. If sitting in a chair, feel your feet on the floor. Inhale and lengthen your spine. Imagine a string is pulling the top of your head toward the sky. Exhale and reach your tailbone toward the Earth, while maintaining that length in your spine. You can imagine your tailbone is a taproot reaching into the Earth and connecting with the heart of the Earth. Keep your chin parallel to the floor. Continue to breathe easily and naturally.

"Place your tongue on the roof of your mouth and imagine a golden ball in front of your third eye chakra (just above your eyes brows, in the center of forehead). Inhale through your nose, roll the ball over the top of your head (crown chakra), down the spine to your tailbone, Chant in your mind 'Hung' down spine. Exhale through nose, rolling the ball back up the spine, over the head to third eye and chant Sau (sah) -sounds like 'saw' on inhalation." (Sylvia Brallier)

## Why Choose a Tantric Lifestyle?

This chant means, "I am That" or "I am." By chanting this mantra you are affirming your True Self as one with the Earth and the Divine, continuing to balance Shiva and Shakti energy within.

Start by doing this practice for five minutes daily and add more time each time you sit. It has been found that it takes about 20 minutes to relax deeply, so aim for 20 minutes each day.

Including this simple meditation in your daily practice could facilitate activation of kundalini energy.

### Third Eye Meditation

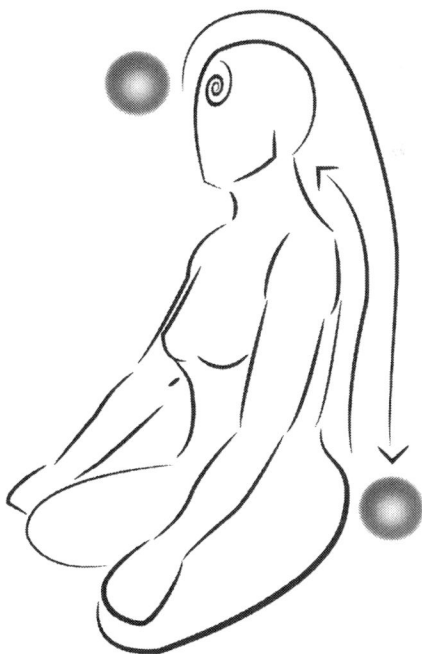

## When Kundalini Energy is Activated

As activation begins, it can be exciting and you may want to play with it. Please do not forget to stay grounded at all times. Try not to control the energy, but instead allow the kundalini to go where it is guided. When the kundalini energy moves around your body, how much can you relax and allow it to flow? If the energy gets stuck and pulsates in one chakra, make sounds, breathe, release emotions that rise and relax deeply. All of these actions can help the energy to move and expand you.

A grounded practice is very important. Once kundalini energy is activated, you may find that a vigorous practice is not serving you anymore because it is making you lightheaded or dizzy, too energized, talkative or you may experience insomnia. If this happens, switch to a gentle and restorative yoga practice, Qigong and meditation. Daily walks in nature also help. You may choose to do weight training for strengthening, as it can be more grounding. Try less movement. Eating grounding foods also helps to bring one down to Earth. Choose root vegetables and foods with oils, like olives and avocados. Massaging oil on your skin after showering is also very grounding. Massage with long strokes along the limbs and in circles on the joints.

Why come down? Because it can be very difficult to function while living in the ethers. When I have lived there, I found that words did not come easily. It was difficult to relate to an average person who is not on a similar path or having similar experiences. If you live and work with others who are not at the same place in their practice, it could be difficult to hold down a job or manage household responsibilities. Kundalini energy can facilitate great focus and clarity, but when not grounded can lead to an airy state of mind, coming across as an "airhead" or "spacey."

Health imbalances can also occur, like insomnia and migraines. I once met a *sangha* (yoga community) member who was experiencing symptoms that resembled Tourette's syndrome. His body would convulse uncontrollably and he would make sounds. His wife had to explain what was going on because he could not carry on a conversation. He essentially became non-functioning. I trust his guru supported him to come into balance. If imbalances occur as the kundalini is healing your body, consult an experienced Tantra educator for support. Emotional clearing and grounding exercises should be provided.

On the upside, senses are enhanced. One feels more, smells more, becomes more sensitive to one's environment and the food taken into one's body temple. One begins to understand what the body needs for optimal health. When the energy channels of the body are clear, communication within the body increases. Clairvoyance increases. The practitioner begins to see their path clearly and does not waver as much about the next steps to creating their intentions. As mentioned earlier, one becomes more focused and passionate. Much can be accomplished when one's kundalini energy is activated, while remaining grounded. Essentially, one is beginning to live their true purpose, and as a result, feels happier and lighter. When one is happier and lighter, one attracts. Attraction leads to success!

**Possible symptoms of kundalini energy that is out of balance:**

- You talk too much and after talking you feel drained.
- Insomnia
- Migraines
- Anxiety
- Tension in muscles due to anxiety, like tight shoulders and neck.
- High energy and extreme depletion cycle after using energy.
- Merging with others' energy field, overly empathetic, unclear boundaries

CHAPTER TWO

# Self Love

When the energy centers (chakras) within the body begin to open in sacred and supportive space, one can become childlike — wide-eyed, excited, quick to laugh and also vulnerable. This is the pure state one is in before experiencing any stress of trauma. After this rebirthing of your true identity, it is time to re-parent yourself in a way that supports your true purpose to thrive.

Many of us, as very young children, were not protected, abused, or raised to behave in ways the culture finds appropriate but which are not authentic for us. These lessons about "how to be" come from our peers, schools and family members.

For example, when I was five years old, I clearly remember saying out loud, "I hate money and clothes." It was because I had been told more than once to put on clothes or that I couldn't do something because we did not have the money. This is one of the first memories I have of my spirit being shut down; when my light started to dim. Somehow maintaining a semblance of inner power after a very disempowering childhood, I spent much of my adult life getting very little use out of a bathing suit and being sure there was always enough money to support my true nature to thrive.

When we are not protected or supported, body parts begin to contract around emotions. This is the body's way of protecting itself from harm. Notice when you become activated by someone else's actions, when you feel hurt. Notice where that shows up in your body and how your body responds. Shoulders rolled forward, protecting the heart chakra, can result from grief or love loss. Intestinal problems, involving the second chakra, can become chronic because of fear or trauma. Shortness of breath is very common in this culture because many are in a chronic state of fear — such as a fear of job loss or of not being good enough. Sexual abuse often shows up in the first and second chakras as a lack of feeling in the pelvis. These are just a few of the more common symptoms I see among clients that have resulted from feeling unsupported or not protected in being themselves. Those who are already practicing yoga may be getting glimpses of their true nature and are nurturing it to thrive.

# Chakra Diagram

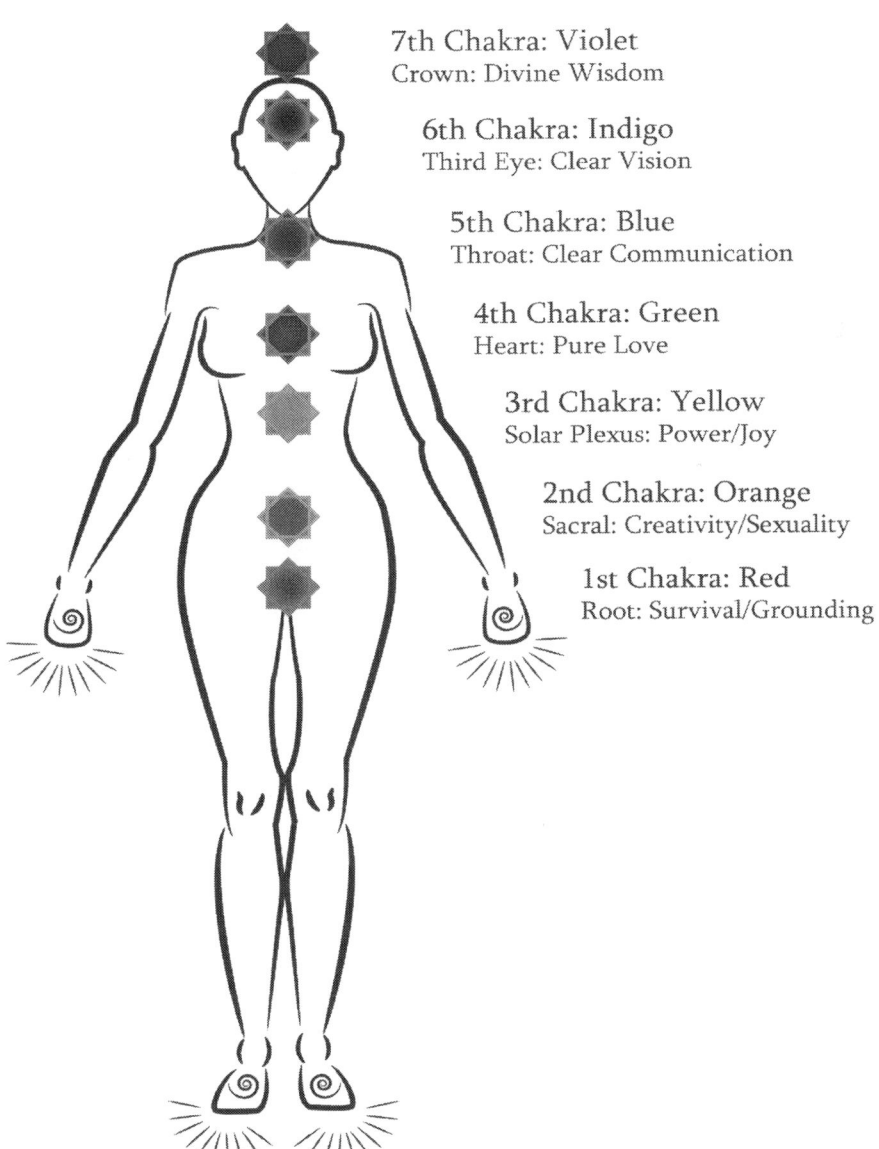

7th Chakra: Violet
Crown: Divine Wisdom

6th Chakra: Indigo
Third Eye: Clear Vision

5th Chakra: Blue
Throat: Clear Communication

4th Chakra: Green
Heart: Pure Love

3rd Chakra: Yellow
Solar Plexus: Power/Joy

2nd Chakra: Orange
Sacral: Creativity/Sexuality

1st Chakra: Red
Root: Survival/Grounding

The body naturally wants to protect itself. Our inner spirit is strong and it wants to survive. So how do you protect your soul to thrive as an adult? By "re-parenting" yourself in healthy ways that do not cause contractions in the body. You practice Self Love.

## Acknowledge your body as your temple.

"You are what you eat." How many times have we heard this expression? So much so that it is ignored? This expression is so true that it even goes beyond food and includes the energy that goes into the food preparation. For example, how well the farmers and land are treated, the ethics of the store in which it was purchased, the attitude of the cook and the atmosphere in the restaurant where it is being served.

**Eat local and organic foods as much as possible.** Start by purchasing organic produce that, when conventionally grown, is known to contain the most pesticide residue, like apples, strawberries and potatoes. I have been eating organic since I was 19 years old, while putting myself through college and as a single mother. Eating organic and local foods can be challenging, but making excuses will not help you find solutions. It is possible and needs to be one's top priority in order to experience overall health and well-being. Food is fuel, and its byproducts, like pesticide residue, add to the body's workload. Food raised in monoculture settings does not provide the same vitality. Food shipped from afar loses its nutritional value over time. We are also learning of the lack of nutrition in genetically modified foods, which are now heavily present in the average supermarket and restaurant. Feed yourself organic and local foods. You will feel the difference. You are worth it! When we make health a priority, the money to buy organic and local shows itself. One summer, one of my students gave me the extra produce from his garden each week after class. I saved about $20 a week as a result of his *seva* (selfless service). When it's needed and you are doing your best, the Universe provides.

**Place your body in healthy situations.** Share your precious time with people who are on the same path, such as those who are not putting poison in themselves, like cigarettes, excessive alcohol, toxic foods or drugs; and those who get adequate sleep, and are also surrounded by healthy friends and colleagues. Choose to work and connect in settings where people are communicating in healthy ways. Acknowledge that we are all in different places on this path, while also recognizing those who are committed to creating a healthy and supportive lifestyle. They are out there and growing in numbers. It takes some discipline to say "no" to situations that do not serve your true purpose. There may be periods of loneliness or transition until you find the right friends and create a supportive work environment. You will be admired for the clear communication used to create a healthy environment where you can thrive.

**Connect with nature every day.** We are a part of the Earth and she keeps us in a natural rhythm. This natural rhythm is essential for maintaining optimal health and remaining grounded and connected to yourself. Remaining grounded and connected to Self will help you to maintain this state in a consistent way, rather than wavering between who you are and who you are expected to be.

I know there are some readers who don't consider themselves the nature type. Find a way to incorporate nature into your life that is comfortable for you. Fill your home and office with plants and flowers. Let your skin be immersed in ocean or spring-fed water. Let your bare feet touch the Earth at the beach or in a garden. In the winter, take walks in the snow. The snow is part of the Earth's atmosphere and you will make a connection. Live in places where the air is clean. It's all a choice. Those who choose to live in big, polluted cities for the money or for other reasons know what I am talking about. They stay with us in Maine every summer for the fresh air. It's a trade off, and many are finding ways to create the balance between earning money, responsibilities to others and health in their lives. It is possible.

**Practice Qigong.** *Qigong* is a movement system that is based in Traditional Chinese Medicine; I discuss specific Qigong exercises in later chapters of this book. A Qigong practice creates a powerful connection with Sky and Earth. Because Qigong motion is mostly downward, it is a very Earthy/Yin/Feminine practice. Qigong is meant to be practiced outdoors, so practice in parks and at the beach or in your yard, pulling energy from all directions, plants, animals and all the elements: Earth, Fire, Water, Metal and Wood.

**Make fires in your home fireplace or in a fire pit in your yard.** Connecting with the element of Wood and warming your body with it brings one closer to the Earth and its elements. You can also burn thoughts in the fire — those thoughts that no longer serve you and that you are choosing to release. Always express gratitude for the tree that gave its life to warm and transform you.

**Choose or design your home** so the windows of the rooms you spend the most time in are facing gardens, water and trees (e.g., rooms like your kitchen, living room, home office or studio). You can do your indoor practice in front of these windows, accessing the grounding and balancing support of nature. Let it teach and guide you to live in balance with Sky and Earth energy.

**Do your best not to let technology consume you**, even though it has become easy and is often a job requirement to stay up to date with it.

Practice maintaining your natural rhythm as technology, and all its layers, call you to speed up. Notice your breath, your posture. Come into a comfortable upright position and breathe easily and naturally while completing your tasks. Take breaks to stretch, move, soak up the sun and fresh air. See how much you can decrease your use of technology and maintain your natural rhythm.

These are just a few of the most important ways to begin creating a safe and supportive container for your True Self to thrive.

## Lifestyle Suggestions for Creating the Life You Are Meant to Live

**Practice Gratitude.** Before launching into a path of Self Love, begin with gratitude. Gratitude is the key to success and will set you free. When one acknowledges that one already has optimal health, a job, a roof over one's head, food, clothes, the mind immediately shifts to abundance and one's entire being can then align with what it is meant to create. Before asking for more, always express genuine gratitude for what you already have and experience.

**Tell the Story you are Creating.** Let go of unsupportive beliefs, patterns, behaviors and addictions by not telling stories about them as if they were in the present. Release the unsupportive parts of your past. A symbolic way to release that which no longer serves you is to write down each thing on a piece of paper and burn it in a fire.

Discipline yourself to tell the story you are choosing. Be clear and precise. No limits. Start with gratitude.

**Create a solid and supportive foundation** that includes service, integrity, accountability, a sense of place or "home" and organized finances.

Aspire to live in the positive financially, or create the ability to finance debt with investment savings. Choose investments that yield the highest interest and are secure. Seek out a reputable financial adviser if you need guidance in this area (most of us do).

## Clean up relationships by:

- Practicing forgiveness.
- Being open to change in others.
- Communicating your needs clearly and lovingly.
- Listening to the needs of others and reflecting their words back to them when you speak (i.e., "active listening").
- Agreeing to disagree or come to a mutual agreement. Enter into disagreements with the intention to get along, by understanding each other's wants and needs, verses trying to be right or to "win."

**Repetition/routine** helps us to stay on track while we create a new behavior. When you feel stuck and are not making progress toward your intentions, change your routine. Feeling stuck is often a sign that it is time to grow and expand. Breathe through resistance to routine. Make a commitment to explore something for at least 30 days. Changing old behaviors happens in stages. Choose new behaviors to adopt that lead to satisfying results. This requires commitment and discipline.

**Ways to stay on track:** Use reminders, notes to Self, accountability to Self. Acknowledge the baby steps. Notice. Reward yourself for accomplishments.

Use this affirmation as needed, whenever you feel you are being influenced by unsupportive people or environments: "As I create a sacred vessel of my body and home, I can remain centered and grounded and do not allow outside influences to throw me off track."

## Creating a Sacred Vessel

Eat just the right foods that your body needs. Notice which foods give you natural energy (vitality) and which foods make you feel tired.

Create a toxin-free home. Research how to create a toxin-free home online.

Live in a location that has a minimal amount of toxins in the environment.

Choose friends that do not require a lot of your emotional energy, but who contribute to your life. In other words, choose friends who are helping themselves and who inspire you — people who enrich your life.

Clear others' energy from your home and personal items. That includes clutter. Clutter is very unsettling and creates a constant reminder to do, do, do. For those who are good at ignoring clutter, it also holds old energy and can leave you stuck in the past, in old patterns. It is best to clear your environment and only place items in it that inspire your current intentions.

Communicate your needs for space clearly and lovingly, so you get just the right amount of rest and alone time that you need to recharge.

Create a balance of giving and receiving. As a health practitioner, I find that when I receive more than I give, I perform better and do not get depleted from my work and service. For example, receiving massages, spa treatments, buying clothes that make me feel good, down time, outings that nourish me rather than deplete me, etc. We each have our own individual capacity to give and receive. Tuning into when you are over-giving and feeling depleted will help you to discern how much is too much.

## Alone Time

Intentional alone time leads to clear intentions. Solo walks, a solo retreat or a private home practice, like yoga, Qigong or meditation, with no time limits, allow us to hear our inner voice and to get clear on where to put our precious energy. Allowing yourself to get bored — that is, not over-busy or constantly distracted — has been known to spur creativity and focus direction.

Always check in with your intention. What are you creating? What are you moving toward? What are your dreams and what is your destiny?

Ask these questions of yourself when alone walking, meditating, journaling, reflecting. Write down your intentions. Create a vision board collage. Place these reminders on your altar or above your mirror, so you look at them daily. One day you may realize you have created some, or all of them, solidly in your life.

As you learn and grow along your path, an intention may not feel true to you anymore. Perhaps you saw that one path was right to receive some lessons, and now a different path is the one to follow. Beware of modality- or teacher-surfing and becoming too scattered. Dive in deep before moving on. Breathe and move through the resistance that surfaces. Often, the resistance is something about yourself that your soul wants to transform.

When your intentions are clear, begin to radiate toward what will help you to create them.

- Supportive and experienced people who are engaged in what you are exploring.

- Resources that will support your intentions.
- Environments that support your vitality and ability to be your best.
- Practice visualizing what you are creating.
- Parent yourself with daily positive affirmation. Tell the story you are creating. Leave out the rest.
- Maintain your daily practice and lifestyle intentions for clear pathways in your life. Be grateful. Love. Forgive.

## Establish a Daily Practice

Your daily practice is a solo path. Although it is important to receive experienced guidance, no one else can do your practice for you. No one can expand your chakras until you are willing to heal the contractions within your energy body. Choose to confront your past and learn to accept it in a new way, one that does not continue to harm you physically and emotionally.

How to create a daily practice?

Pick a location and set it up for practice. This space should be clean and clear with pictures and altar items that reflect your intentions. It should also be quiet, with minimal distractions and no electronics.

Electronics affect the energy around you and raise the vibration higher than what is a natural rhythm. Electronics can make one tense and irritable and that is counterproductive to what one is choosing to experience through spiritual practice.

Your practice is a time to be alone and reflect. It is a time to tune in to your body, mind and spirit and allow it to send clear messages that will support your path. This is a subtle experience and requires deep inward awareness, which is cultivated through repetition.

Begin by noticing the breath and clearing the mind. One can study with master teachers to learn practices like meditation, movement, chanting, breathing exercises and more. You can also begin with my podcasts, *Self Love: Guided Visualization and Gentle and Restorative Flows,* which include photos of poses and are free on our website www.tantratolove.com. I include a sample of practices in this book to help you get started. Books do not replace, but are meant to supplement, in-person study.

Practices are given to our private students based on individual needs for opening and clearing tensions in the energy body. We encourage the use of sound as a way to vibrate open the body, as well as shamanic shaking. We spend a lot of time practicing variations on the theme of *savasana*, the corpse pose, by practicing "the art of dying" and deep surrender. When one learns to let go completely, life becomes much easier to negotiate and bliss is revealed. When one allows the past to die, one invites in new, fresh and positive opportunities. If one continues to choose to hold onto the past, those old wounds will follow and express themselves in all one's actions and interactions.

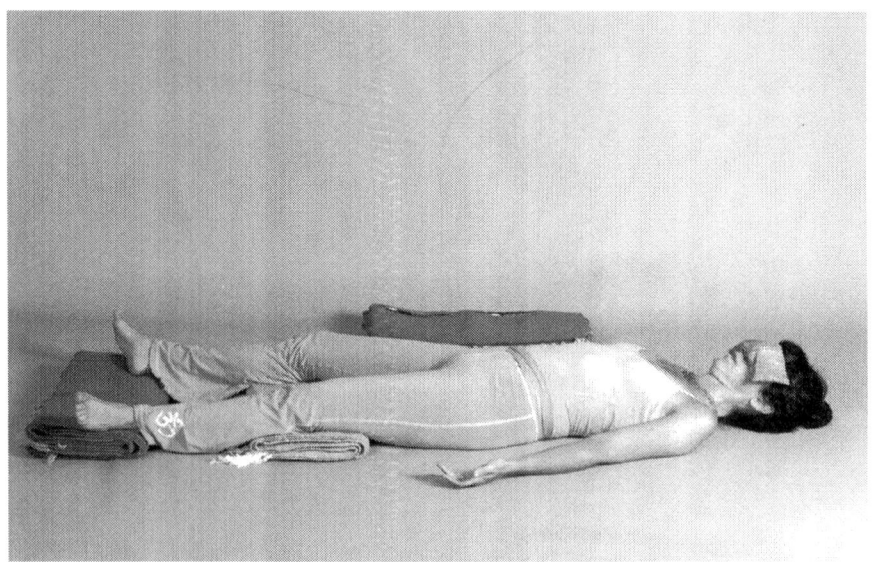

"Savasana"

To deepen the practice and to overcome any obstacles, we invite our students to feel fully and to express their emotions through private Phoenix Rising Yoga Therapy sessions. We assist our students in relearning how to relax and receive with therapeutic massage.

Eventually, your practice becomes "home": a place where you can go, be yourself and find peace. You may notice that when you skip a day, your mood is different. Your body may feel tense. Your language may not be as loving. Your practice keeps you on track with your intentions: the path you are now choosing.

Below are two foundational practices you can begin learning immediately. The first is from Qigong, the other from tantric yoga.

### Qigong Organ Clearing

I begin my daily practice with this Qigong movement. It assists in clearing unwanted energy and in bringing fresh qi into the body. It is also an excellent practice before connecting with another person, or before going to a party or into an unsupportive environment where there may be a lot of challenging personalities or activities – like an amusement park or a big city. You can view this movement series on my YouTube channel www.youtube.com/PranaHeals

1. Stand in "horse stance": position your knees wider than your hips with knees bent deeply, and turn knees out to create a "U" shape in your groin area. Be sure to keep your knees over your feet.

2. Shift your weight from side to side, feeling all the points on the bottoms of your feet in that direction. Bring your feet to stillness. Shift your weight forward and back, feeling all the points on the bottoms of your feet in that direction. Bring the feet to stillness. Lift the toes, spread them apart, and then lower them. Make a connection with the Bubbling Well, the acupuncture kidney point between the ball of the big toe and the pad of the other toes, and the floor or Earth.

3. Rub your palms together. Clap your hands a few times. Gently bend each finger back to open the palms.

4. Place your arms out to your sides, palms facing up. Inhale and lift the arms, gathering universal qi from all around you. It is recommended to practice Qigong outdoors or to look out a window and gather energy from the rocks, trees, plants and animals around you, embodying these aspects of nature: how a tree is rooted, how a plant moves in the wind, the delicate nature of a flower, the solidity of a rock.

5. When palms are overhead, turn them downward and soften the top of your head. Exhale and imagine you are raining white light through your head, face, neck and shoulders, and through your torso and the organs within your torso as you slowing bring your palms down and in front of your body, guiding the qi. As you do this, imagine your body being cleansed and filled with white light, clearing away any tensions, toxins or allergens.

6. Place you palms in front of your pelvis and imagine placing all the good, clean energy there. Imagine all the tensions, toxins and allergens flowing through your legs, out your feet and into the Earth, to be composted into pure energy.

7. Repeat five times for the five elements: Earth, Fire, Water, Metal and Wood.

8. After repeating this clearing movement five times, circulate the clean energy three times by repeating the same movement described above, but a bit quicker. Inhale the arms up and exhale the arms down.

9. Place palms on belly, below navel. Right palm down first for women and left palm down first for men.

### Three-Part Yogic Breath (Standing Wave Yoga)

This is a very calming *pranayama* practice. It is a Tantra technique that I suggest mastering at the beginning of your Tantra studies. By learning this breath, you will create balance and spaciousness within the chakra system and be able to manage any kundalini energy experiences or imbalances.

It is described below, and I also teach it at the beginning of the Gentle Flow in my *Self Love* podcast that can be downloaded for free at www.tantratolove.com

1. While lying on your back in savasana, let your knees and feet fall to the sides, with your feet about 8-12 inches apart. Arms by your side about six inches away from the body.

2. Inhale your right palm to your abdomen, just below your navel, and as you exhale, soften your elbow and shoulder down so they are touching the floor.

3. Inhale your left palm to your upper chest and exhale your elbow and shoulder down so they are touching the floor.

4. Inhale into your belly, filling your belly, then ribs, then upper chest with fresh air.

5. Press the left palm down slightly and exhale from the upper chest, then ribs, then abdomen, pulling the abdomen in slightly to release any stale air.

6. Continue repeating this sequence, seeing how much you can lengthen your breath and slow your breath down.

7. Once you feel you have mastered this breathing technique, as you exhale, you can float your palms down to your sides about six inches away from the body, palms up.

8. Continue three-part yogic breathing without using your hands as a guide. Internalizing this breath. Fully oxygenate your body and completely release all the stale air, allergens and toxins.

You may choose to keep your palms on your body, as this can be very centering and self-nurturing.

I often use this breathing technique to help me fall asleep or to calm me during stressful times.

You can also use it when you feel any tension in your chakra system. Breathe deep into the tension and release with a complete exhale. Sound also helps as a form of release. You can sigh, groan or make a low tone to release with sound. In Phoenix Rising Yoga Therapy, we call this a "falling out breath."

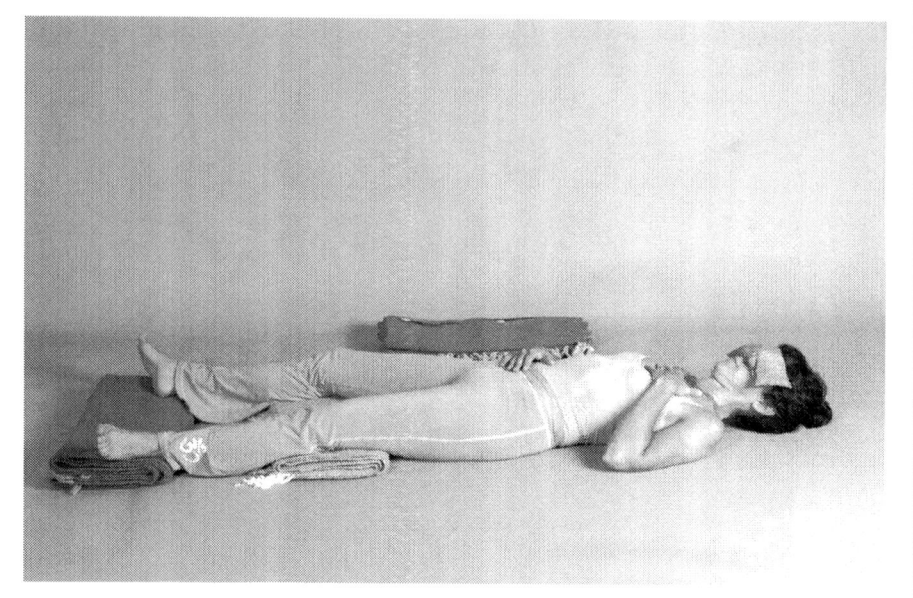

"Three Part Yogic Breathing"

CHAPTER THREE

# Transforming Ego

Freudian psychology says the ego lies between the conscious and unconscious (Snowden, 2006). Jungian psychology proposes the idea that there are two centers of the personality. The ego is the center of consciousness, whereas the Self is the center of the total personality, which includes consciousness, the unconscious, and the ego (Zweig, 1991). The ego is our inner child screaming for love and attention. It is the part of us that needs to be fed with new things and new sensations. The ego is what brings most people to Tantra: to experience a better — or a "wilder" — sex life. Sorry to disappoint, but that will not happen until the ego is transformed; when one can bring the unconscious parts of the psyche to the surface to be honored and accepted, allowing oneself to be vulnerable and open to expand oneself and share energy with another.

So how do you go about transforming your ego? Well, this is a lifelong journey, so don't be hard on yourself if it doesn't happen right away. Transforming the ego takes courage. It takes courage to be nothing, to be nobody — just to be and exist without recognition. This goes against how we are raised in developed nations. Instead, we are raised to compete and succeed, and those actions in themselves can require having a big ego. Psyching yourself up for success. Affirming, "I do this well (or not)."

The desire for success is often very ego-driven. It means, "I can't live with myself unless I have a big house, a new car, trendy furniture and clothing." Until the attachment to all of that is released, the ego will not completely transform.

Contrary to what you may be thinking, Tantra practitioners can end up being very successful. When taking the journey of stripping away the ego, the traveler becomes authentic and reveals their true Self, their true identity. When one lives an honest and authentic life, one feels more relaxed because one is not trying to be someone they are not. You feel happier because you are actually doing what you want to do and not what is expected. Happy people attract. Attraction leads to success.

So how can you release the attachment to being successful and simply trust that you will be provided for when living an authentic and honest life?

Tantra teaches us to have a strong sense of Self and clear boundaries, so if you sense you are being taken advantage of, speak up or walk away from that relationship. Through practice, one's intuition becomes very sensitive and aware when a situation is not ethical or safe. Instead, choose to align with those who are also living honest and authentic lives.

How do we do this as a Tantra practice? Well, the physical practice of yoga is a great place to start. Ignore all the pictures you see in the media of yogis doing backbends and handstands. Instead, surrender to each pose. Start at the beginning. Accept your body where it is in this moment, with all its tightness caused by physical and emotional history. Most of the pictures of yogis that we see in the media are of dancers, gymnasts or those who practice in hot yoga studios for many years. That is not the beginning and may not ever be your end goal. If you are starting a yoga practice later in life, you may have experienced many years of holding the body in ways that protect you. This all needs to be undone. So consider how many years it took your body to become less flexible and put that much time, focus and attention into your yoga practice. Even if you are never able to do a backbend or handstand, you will be transformed and feel so much better. You will feel open and cleansed of all the old emotions that you were holding in your muscles and joints. So by letting go of needing to look like those pictures in the media, you are transforming your ego.

Now you can bring this into your daily life. How much can you surrender to those whom you are close to — your family, friends and coworkers? Do you always need to get your way? Can you completely release ownership of your ideas, or at least find ways to collaborate and combine your ideas with others? Can you surrender to a communication practice that will get you to this place of collaboration? Can you surrender to not always being right? As I will mention further in the chapter on communication, you may find that it feels better to surrender than to be right. You may experience more peace, rather than the solitude people sometimes experience when they force their ideas onto others. How much can you listen and collaborate?

Surrender is a major step in transforming ego.

What are you transforming your ego into? Well, love, of course!

How much can you feel compassion for others and truly love them unconditionally, even when they are hurting you? This is where the lifelong journey comes in. I can't say I am always there at almost 50 years old, and after more than 30 years of practice. I still have personal healing and practice to do around this. We all have our own personal emotional history. Healing childhood wounds takes place in a timeframe that is not in our control. It happens in divine timing as the body, mind and spirit can integrate it over a lifetime — or lifetimes. This healing takes place as you love yourself enough to give yourself what you need to heal; not only by making your healing your top priority, but also by loving yourself in ways that you may not have been loved as a child. Protect yourself from the not-so-loving souls still finding their way, while you stay open and loving. Sometimes, this means removing yourself from hurtful situations or people.

The journey starts here, and when you feel grounded and strong enough, then you can begin to collaborate and create with just about anyone. When you can do this, that is when success will really begin to flow in your life: when you heal yourself and are capable of healing with others; when you can understand another's perspective and communicate your perspective lovingly and free of attachment. Trusting that there are others doing the same and that in time, with persistence, things will change for the better. Light can overcome darkness. When you really think about it, who is attracted to someone with a big ego? It is actually repelling, isn't it? And it is indicative of deeper insecurities.

Let those operating from an ego mindset get their own lessons. In the meantime, you can continue to cultivate love in your being and, as a result, attract more and more love and success into your life.

My husband Rene is a great real-life example. He had a relatively unscathed childhood. He was heavily supported and loved. He was never afraid to make friends, despite a move in high school. He was class vice president, funny and popular. He had to work hard in school to gain his credentials, but is mostly known for his personality and ability to negotiate relationships. As a result, work opportunities come to him. He does not need to seek them out. He is known for his competence, but most of all, his ability to get along with others. His gift has become one of relationship negotiator, so whenever we have a situation that needs negotiating in our school and private practice, I hand it over to Rene. I am still healing my childhood wounds and get very activated by conflict. He coasts right through conflict and has no trouble with surrender. He finds common ground and most people leave the situation feeling heard.

We all have our own journey to walk with transforming our egos. Give yourself the time and space that is needed and notice how your life changes.

> For thousands of years, Tantra practitioners have known that chanting mantras can change thought patterns in the brain. Science has now documented this phenomena called nueroplasty. Essentially, the nueropathways in the brain can change and the brain can grow by thinking new and repetitive thoughts. Health practitioners are now using nueroplasty as a way to improve memory, brain health and to change beliefs systems. (Pat Lind-Kyle, 2010)
>
> In my experience as a *sangha* (community member) in a Kashmir Shaivism based ashram, I noticed the chant "Om Namah Shivaya" was given to new students. It is meant to be embodied by regular practice before practicing any new mantras. If students request to practice a new mantra, master teachers (*swamis*) evaluate whether the students is well on the path of transforming their ego. Mantras are then given to students as they are drawn to certain *deities*. Deities are a major part of the Kashmir Shaivism tradition and are simply role models who guide us. Each *deity* has a story and aspects of their personality that assist the Tantra practitioner in meeting daily challenges. Well known deities are Ganesh, remover of obstacles. A statue of Ganesha is found on the dashboards of cars and rickshaws in India. Lakshmi is also a popular one who assists us in being prosperous and healthy.

Lighter: Living Tantra

> By chanting "Om Namah Shivaya" as a regular practice, one receives divine assistance to release ego derived thoughts and behaviors. By choosing to chant this mantra, one becomes more aware when the ego crops up in life and one can chose to change that behavior to something more humble. A popular way to chant this mantra is on mala beads by passing one mala bead at a time through you thumb and fore finger. I like to chant myself to sleep.

CHAPTER FOUR

# Clear, Honest and Loving Communication

In order to keep the chakra system open and, consequently, the energy flowing throughout the body for optimal health, I recommend the practice of open, honest and loving communication. When one holds one's truth inside, the body contracts in certain areas of the chakra system. Many of my clients feel this constriction in their throat and sometimes in their abdominal area. They often describe the feeling in their second and third chakras (abdominal region) as "upset" or "knotted." Some even experience digestive problems like irritable bowel syndrome. In other cases, when emotionally charged words are spoken, constriction in the vocal cord area is audible. Do you notice areas in your life where you may not have a voice, such as at work, or in your relationships? Often there is a trauma in one's past that had activated this pattern.

Michael Lee, founder of Phoenix Rising Yoga Therapy and author of *Turn Stress into Bliss*, has seen in his experience that,

> … certain *"ways of being present to life" cause energy to flow in different ways. Sometimes this habitual "distortion" of the flow of energy can create aberrations in body and mind and can also create a separation from one's spirit. This could be called "dis-ease",*

*but that is only one of many possible manifestations of one's presence to life being out of whack with one's truth.*

Communication becomes an essential skill for lasting intimacy. Clearing the chakra system of past traumas that affect communication is a good first step in developing this skill. This can be done with a trained Phoenix Rising Yoga Therapist or other professional trained in somatic (mind/body) emotional clearing.

The next step is quite simple. Below I provide communication techniques that can be learned quickly. Once learned, all that is required is a commitment to practice and use these skills, rather than going back to old ways of communicating.

## How To Get Started

- Take the time to communicate.
- Take the solo time you need to breathe through any raw emotions. Communicate when you can be calm and less attached to the outcome. Receive support (e.g., counseling or emotional clearing) if needed.
- Remember that the intention of clear, honest and loving communication is to get along.
- Focus on the other person's feelings and needs. We all want to be heard and understood.
- Identify your role in creating the conflict before you begin to resolve it. Come to conflict resolution with humility. Begin sharing your needs by using the word "I." For example, "I feel upset, sad and angry when I experience (fill in the blank).
- Stay away from "the story." Rehashing it does not serve anyone and, often, shared stories are perceived differently by each individual involved. Clarifying "the story" can get you into a long,

drawn-out discussion that will, most likely, lead to agreeing to disagree. Instead, keep it simple.
- How lovingly can you communicate your feelings and needs without blaming? Let go of ego and the need to pass blame, even if blame makes you feel better. By releasing ego and attachment, notice the conflict begin to slip away. Life becomes more easeful.
- Give all involved an opportunity to fully express their feelings and needs. Listen and reflect back exactly what you are hearing.

In our workshops and private sessions, we share a dialog technique that is a step-by-step approach to communicating. It includes examples of non-activating words that can be used to express needs and feelings. This technique has proven to be very effective. My husband Rene and I use it all the time when we begin to argue. Sometimes, we can hear that we are in a power struggle and not listening to each other's feelings and needs. When that happens, usually one of us stops arguing and asks to dialogue. When others feel heard and understood, and don't experience a need to win or lose the argument, conflict dissolves.

CHAPTER FIVE

# Community, Companionship and Partnership

It's not about the body. Tantra invites us to rise above the body.

Separate from the body and let your spirit fly free. The spirit has so much power, way beyond what the body can physically hold.

Life is a solo journey. In order to access the power of your soul, you need to get to know it.

## What about companionship and community?

This is where one can get lost. When we spend too much time in a group or partnership, we can lose track of who we are as an individual. This happens very easily in schools and the workplace. So much of one's quality hours are spent there, often following rules and a way of behaving and thinking that were created by others.

It is important to take significant time alone, checking in with what feels nourishing for your soul's growth and potential.

What I have discovered is that it is best to look at life as a solo journey, where we focus mostly on Self. This includes nourishing our body temple and destiny, with ongoing awareness of and sensitivity to how our actions affect others and the planet. Individuals can come together and move apart as needed, so that each individual can access their highest potential as Self and for the planet as a whole, including all life forms, air, soil and water. Imagine we are all standing in X pose (shown in Chapter Seven, page 54), expanded and connected to each other and the planet.

Nurture Self, your soul, and fly!

Come together for connection and support, creating a "patchwork quilt" of support (as described by Sylvia Brallier), free of expectations of others.

If you are ill and need support, when you have healthy moments, create a support network of practitioners and people who can assist you. If healthy moments are rare for you, ask a loved one or friend for assistance in creating this network. If you are in financial need, there are services available to assist you. True healers will not turn you away because of money. An energy exchange is always a good idea. It keeps your energy field clear, so you do not feel tied to anyone, creating ongoing feelings that you owe people. If you believe in karma, in this lifetime or another, you may find yourself in a position to pay it back someday.

---

**When the body is in pain, meditate.**

Ask for support from your angels, guides and ancestors.

Invite your crown chakra to soften and open.

---

> Breathe divine healing energy into the parts of the body in pain. Imagine you are breathing open the top of your head, release thoughts and any efforting, and gently guide your breath into your body. First, guide the breath into the body part that is calling your attention to it. Continue bringing your breath and awareness there, until you feel clear, relaxed and open (vs. contracted).
>
> Move to the next part of your body that is now calling your attention and repeat until your whole body feels lighter and healthier – possibly even pain free!

## Healthy Ways to Connect and Live in Community

As humans, we are drawn to each other for safety (as primitive mammals, we found safety in numbers) and love. We are drawn to each other for inspiration, camaraderie and companionship. Connection also helps us to create big dreams and expand our vision worldwide. Many positive changes have occurred because of group efforts. Connection and community are necessary and important. Even those who have reached their limit with others and are choosing a life of isolation may find the need for connection and community at some point in their life, when the journey becomes too big for one person to handle. In the book and movie *Into the Wild* (a true story), the main character chose to live a very isolated life in Alaska. Before dying of starvation, he came to the realization that one can only experience true happiness when it is shared. In the yogic traditions, we believe that true happiness can only be found within. In any case, there is a longing to share this happiness with others. The vibration of joy has the potential to be raised exponentially when shared. The same goes for creating global change.

**How can we connect and live in community in a way that is nourishing, uplifting and productive?**

Create equal energy exchanges. If you are still learning how to manifest financial resources, determine other ways you can give your time and the resources that you do have. Remember that summer I was fed by my student's abundant garden? That translated into a financial savings for me.

Live free of expectations. When one expects others to provide a certain type or amount of support, one can often end up disappointed. When one lives free of expectations, one may be pleasantly surprised by what is received. When free of expectations, one begins to see the abundance that is always present and accessible.

When you see ways you can support one another, go for it! When the connection begins to drag down or slow your progress toward your intentions in an unproductive way, reevaluate the connection. Perhaps it has served its purpose and it is now time to move down your path alone for a while. We attract people for different reasons. Those who are meant to connect will.

Say positive things about others. When we keep it positive, everyone feels better and no one is a recipient of negative energy. It may feel good in the moment to blame or criticize, however, it brings everyone down to a lower vibration. Instead, let's raise each other up.

How can you help connect others? Be aware of the web of connections you are creating. Welcome others into it to support one another's varying interests and creative projects.

Take significant time alone to nourish Self. Be at your best when connecting with others. Conscious connection requires awareness and energy. Come to connection rested and nourished on all levels, physically and emotionally. This way, you have something to give to the group and are not just there to receive. Also, if a challenging moment occurs, like a miscommunication, you will be grounded, centered and able to be your best in that situation.

## Practice Conscious Communication (see Chapter Four)

**Model Self Love**, so others learn how to do the same. When you love your Self that much, others may label you as "selfish." They may even be jealous of you for creating such a healthy and abundant life. Find friends and co-workers who are doing the same. Instead of feeling jealousy, support each other in living healthy lives and your highest potentials. There will always be those who do not feel empowered enough to choose a similar path. Send them love and compassion and continue to live the life that brings you the most rewards — the riches that really matter, like health and love.

> *People are often unreasonable, irrational, and self-centered; forgive them anyway. If you are kind, people may accuse you of selfish, ulterior motives: Be kind anyway. What you spend years creating others could destroy overnight: Create anyway. If you find serenity and happiness, some may be jealous. Be happy anyway. The good you do today, will often be forgotten. Do good anyway. Give the best you have, and it may never be enough: Give your best anyway. In the final analysis, it is between you and God: it was never between you and them anyway.*
>
> *~Mother Teresa*

### Practice Forgiveness

While alone, picture a person who may have harmed you and say all you have to say to her about the wrongdoing. Acknowledge her past and find compassion for the healing she stills need to do. Send her off with love to find her way on her own. Energetically separate from her. I often envision I am cutting cords with a large set of scissors. I cut the energetic cords where I feel tension in my body when I think of that person. Push her away with one hand, and then push your other hand into yourself. Feel the separation between the two of you. You may need to do this exercise several times until you do not feel an emotional charge when you think of that person.

You can also chant the ancient Hawaiian ho'oponopono prayer below. In time, the charge will dissipate. It is your job not to rehash the old wound over and over. That reactivates it.

"I'm sorry. Please forgive me. I love you. Thank you."

CHAPTER SIX

# The Shadow and How it Plays into Getting Along with Others

In this chapter, I will define the shadow side of our personality, how to notice it and how to learn from it. The shadow side of the personality is what seems to cause us to struggle in life. With awareness of the shadow, one can learn to transform this aspect of Self to a lighter way of being in the world, while experiencing more peace and self-acceptance.

Notice what it is about another person that bothers, annoys or upsets you. When one gets upset, bothered or annoyed by another person's behavior, I call this being "activated," a term I learned from Sandra Boston in her Conscious Communication classes.

If you check in deeply, you may discover that the behavior activating you is something you don't like about yourself. Often this behavior bothers us most when it is being played out in the worst extreme. For example, an individual may have learned to lie as a child to get what she needed. As an adult, she learned that being honest feels better and gets a better response, so now she always tells the truth and goes as far as to insist that everyone in her life is completely honest. When she discovers someone is lying to her, she gets very upset. She may even choose not to be around people who lie, rejecting them from her life. For this reason, she may have difficulty identifying or recognizing her shadow. Nobody likes to see themselves in that light, especially if they have spent many years changing that part of themselves. Ego seems to play a big role in protecting these shadow aspects of Self.

In Jungian psychology, the "shadow" or "shadow aspect" may refer to the entirety of the unconscious, which includes both positive and negative aspects of one's personality.

If we become envious or jealous of others, it may be because deep inside we want to be like them: kind, talented, attractive, generous, wealthy. This aspect of Self can be called the "golden shadow." It is the part of ourselves that has yet to be developed, who we have the potential to grow into, with compassion, awareness and intention.

When we notice jealousy rise within us, we can instead send admiration to the person we are jealous of. Wish that person ongoing success. Watch and learn. Ask questions. Figure out how this person became who they are today. My guess is that it did not come naturally or easily, but with intention, awareness and hard work. Being successful in life (in other words, *attracting*) requires piecing together a complex puzzle of skills, abilities and characteristics. People will come up with reasons to rationalize how someone else became successful (with her good looks, connections, money, etc.). Even when one comes into this life with money, charisma or beauty, skills are also needed to be successful. Money may buy skills easier and faster, but they are not synonymous. Those who gain their skills through loans, scholarships and hard work are often successful because of their strong work ethic and desire to change their lifestyle.

How can one own the shadow parts of Self with deep love and compassion?

It is important to honor that we are all on our own unique path, with our own unique emotional history, to heal in divine time, when we are ready. When one recognizes the shadow within, one is able to hold those who activate us with love and compassion.

Tantra yoga can play a role in integrating the shadow sides of Self by balancing the masculine and feminine traits within. Shiva (Sky energy / the masculine aspect of Self) is where ego lives. Shakti (Earth energy / the feminine aspects of Self) softens ego. Balance of the masculine and feminine aspects of Self, and a consequent tempering of ego, is accomplished with what Rudi Ballentine calls *yang feminine communication,* that is, being "Fearless to speak with love (shiva), free of ego (shakti)." (*Kali Rising*, 2010)

When exploring the shadow aspects of Self, and in your quest to bring them into balance, notice what you need to heal in this situation. Ask yourself, "Why did I attract this person into my life? What have they come to teach me?"

Integrating the shadow sides of Self promotes healthy responses when others behave in a way that is not favorable. It requires deep self-reflection, awareness and compassion. All of that can be achieved with a regular Tantra yoga and Qigong practice that balances masculine and feminine energies within. Developing skills for managing emotions and communicating effectively will also promote inner and outer peace. An awareness of our Shadow parts, and not reacting when they are activated, could go a long way in creating more peace throughout the world.

CHAPTER SEVEN

# Maintaining Your Center and Integrating

Strengthening the core is an essential part of the Tantra to Love™ philosophy of Tantra lifestyle. A strong core, or center, strengthens the solar plexus chakra. This is the third chakra and energy center that is connected to personality and identity. It is also the place where we feel joy. The feeling of joy becomes very evident when living one's true identity. When we are strong in our center, we feel strong being ourselves in the world — communicating clearly and lovingly our needs, so we stay on our true path. When one is open and loving, one attracts and can become overwhelmed by others' requests for help or to connect socially. A strong core allows one to feel strong in one's choices and able to stay true to one's Self.

In my own Tantra education journey, I took a break from applying *bandhas* (locking the energy flow and releasing) during my *asana* (yoga postures) practice. My yoga practice became very soft. This was when I was exclusively practicing Standing Wave yoga. The style is all about surrender and I believe this is an important step in awakening kundalini energy. If the body is not relaxed the kundalini energy will get stuck in the contractions within the body, or may not be able to move at all — especially if the pelvis is contracted. This is where the kundalini awakening begins. The process of surrender and releasing ego allows the kundalini energy to awaken.

After about three years or so of a soft practice, my body structure and energy body began to call for core strengthening and more toning. I continued the soft style of practice, but added weight training. For my body, while managing fibromyalgia, doing a *vinyasa* or *Ashtanga* practice was no longer physically possible without a lot of wrist pain. Instead I found other ways to strengthen the core. Below I will describe a few options to consider as additions to your daily practice.

When practicing yoga, after spending a significant amount of time opening the hips, pelvis, spine and heart center, blend in some core strengtheners, like starfish or head-to-knee pose.

---

**Starfish Pose (Standing Wave Yoga)**

I love Starfish pose because it provides an opportunity to expand and then pull back into Self, a beautiful metaphor for life. When we expand fully in life, we need to take just as much time or more pulling in and taking excellent care of Self. Get the rest your body requires, eat the food that provides the most vitality, and communicate clear and loving boundaries so you have the space you need for your self-care and connection with Self.

Begin Starfish pose by lying on your back. As you inhale, extend you arms and legs out like a starfish: arms in a V shape around head, legs in V shape. Now your body is in an X pose. Including your head makes it a Starfish pose. Raise your arms, legs and head off the floor. Raising your head is optional and not advised for those with neck concerns. Exhale and pull your body into a tight ball in head-to-knee pose. Repeat by expanding the body into starfish as you inhale, then contracting back to head-to-knee pose as you exhale, until you feel like you can't do it anymore. Do it one or two more times, then, on an exhalation, drop your arms and legs to the floor dramatically and gently without hurting yourself. Rest in savasana, also called "corpse pose": lie on your back with your eyes closed; with legs extended, allow knees and feet to fall to the sides, feet about 8-12 inches apart; relax your arms by your sides about six inches away from your body with palms up.

### Head-to-Knee Pose

While lying on your back, after doing a very expansive pose like starfish pose, draw your head to your knees and your knees to your head and wrap your arms around your shins. Breathe into your core, sealing the yoga in your center. Hold for several breaths until you can't hold it any longer. Hold for a few breaths more, then release and rest in savasana.

I also suggest adding *ujai* breathing: inhale and exhale through the nose, while gently constricting the throat, so the breath sounds like you are fogging a mirror. Direct the breath to your core and allow the breath to provide the strength you need to hold the pose.

# Lighter: Living Tantra

"Starfish"

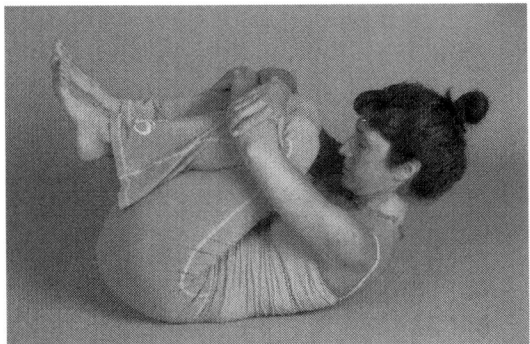

"Head to Knee Pose"

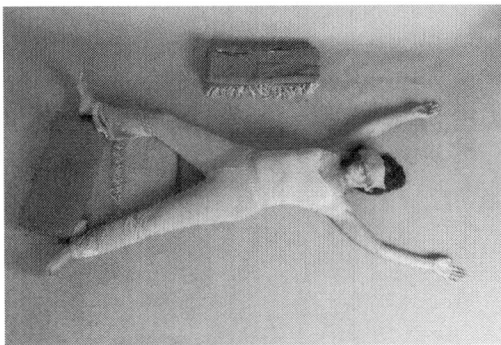

"X Pose"

## Pilates

While managing fibromyalgia, Pilates has become another way that I strengthen my core. After studying it privately for over a year, it became very clear that Joseph Pilates studied yoga and has blended yoga into almost all the Pilates exercises. I also find that Pilates is very tantric. Many of the exercises open the pelvis and upper chest and bring awareness to the spine. The breathing exercises energize, and in my case, activate kundalini energy.

I suggest Pilates for those who are healing from injuries and are not physically able to do a strenuous yoga flow as part your Tantra practice. For those who are injured, the machine and spring-loaded resistance work is particularly beneficial (not everyone knows that Pilates is more than mat work).

Bethany Mateosian, Master Level classical Pilates instructor, says:

> *Because people spend a lot of time sitting, they lose their connection with their core. In Pilates, we instruct our students to move from their center outward in each exercise, retraining the body to come from this deep, powerful place and not have to overuse the neck, low back and hip flexors (front of hip joints) that so often jump in when the core is turned off. Pilates is also a great massage for your internal organs, and often leaves people feeling refreshed and energized.*

## Engaging the *Bandhas*

If you are able to do sun salutations, when doing so, engage the *mula bandha* and *uddiyana bandha*. *Bandhas* are "body locks," or ways of contracting three specific areas of the body. We sometimes engage bandhas during yoga asana and pranayama practice to seal energy (*prana*/life force) in the body for a certain amount of breaths. Once the breath is released, energy moves from the center of the contraction (body lock) to the other parts of the body. Relaxation is such an important part of asana practice because releasing contraction allows the energy to move throughout the body to promote healing and balance. In this section, I will share the three main *bandhas* used in yoga. They are *mula bandha, uddiyana bandha* and *jalandhara bandha*.

I only recommend engaging the bhandas as a part of your Tantra yoga practice and discourage it as an exclusive practice. In my *Ashtanga* studies (all *vinyasa* styles originated from *Ashtanga*), students are encouraged to engage the *mula bandha* throughout the class. This involves squeezing the perineum, the muscle between the anus and genitals, upward into the center of your body. This action is also encouraged in Pilates.

In my early 30s, I studied *Ashtanga* and strenuous *hatha* styles for many years. I was on my way to creating a *vinyasa* style that blended yoga with dance. My main teacher at the time, Satya Gita Van Dyke, had switched to teaching Standing Wave. I wanted to continue to study with her. Her teaching is so compelling, that although the style is dramatically different, I began studying Standing Wave with her. As I mentioned before, this yoga style is all about surrender. Beginners were asked to do a floor-based flow, done on our backs. I was not shown "air poses" (on knees or standing) until I was "ready," when I had mastered this flow, surrender and releasing of ego. At first the flow was very difficult for me. I was fit, energized and had trouble sitting still. I used breath and sound to release those tensions and soon I felt the benefits of this softer Tantra practice and was hooked.

As I began to open my pelvis, I found that engaging the *mula bandha* became counterproductive. I took a long break from using it, unless I was practicing or teaching pranayama, a particular yoga breathing technique. I reserved it for that.

I encourage you to take the same journey. Begin with a soft hip, heart, pelvis and spine opening practice like Standing Wave. Try my gentle audio podcasts for a Standing Wave style practice. Yoga Nidra, Yin Yoga, Svaroopa or restorative yoga provide a similar experience, but are not focused on the process of kundalini awakening. Attend our workshops to experience Standing Wave style flows, which we have modified while honoring tradition. Standing Wave is a closed yoga community based in Northern California. I was fortunate to be accepted in when it was open to new students. There are a few teachers still sharing it in public classes throughout California.

Engage the *bandhas* only when doing a sun salutation strengthening series (or when practicing pranayama). I suggest sets of one, three or six sun salutations, engaging the *bandhas*.

There are other standing (or "air") poses, where engaging the core is helpful for structural integrity and alignment, like plank and triangle. Whenever your belly is just hanging out there off your spine, engage the *mula bandha* and zip up your abs: imagine there is a zipper that begins at your public bone in the center and front of your pelvis, and zip your abs up to your diaphragm, drawing your navel toward your spine and toward your diaphragm. This is called *uddiyana bandha*.

The last *bandha* lock is *jalandhara bandha,* which involves tucking your chin toward the chest. We only apply all the *bandhas* during pranayama (breathing exercises) by locking the breath in the upper chest, then releasing. This release creates a rush of energy through the body and facilitates kundalini awakening.

In summary, the idea is to keep your core intact, without contracting in the pelvis, anus and genitals. If you feel tension in your genitals, allow them to relax. I have found that some Pilates exercises and practicing *mula bandha* incorrectly can create tension in the genitals. If you do end up creating this tension by doing core work, a good counter-stretch is a bent knee straddle or upward-facing triple diamond.

### Upward-Facing Triple Diamond (Standing Wave Yoga)

Bring the soles of the feet together and heels as far away from the groin as possible. Bring your thumbs and forefingers together and rest the backs of your hands on the floor above your head. Arms make a diamond shape around your head. If this stretch is too intense for your inner thighs, you can place blocks, pillows or blankets under your knees. Soften the groin. Soften your shoulders. Breathe into the stretch.

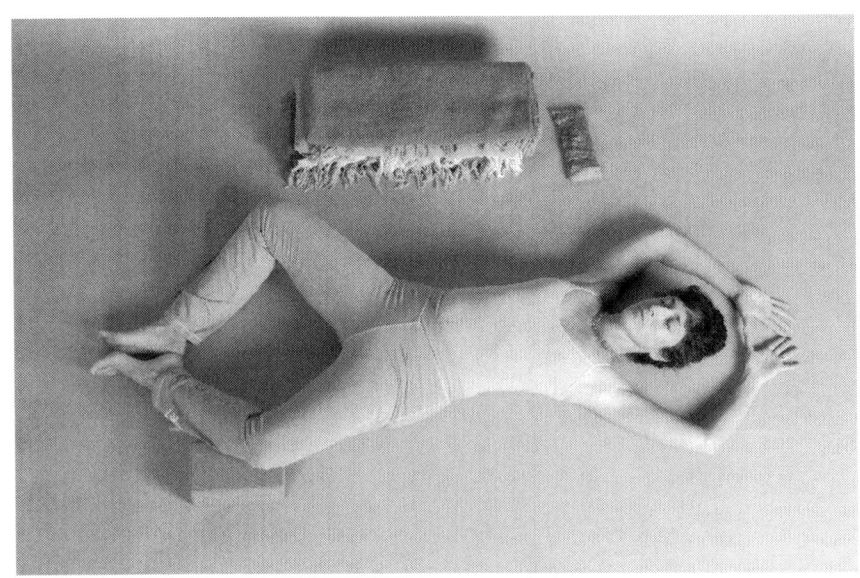

> **Bent Knee Straddle**
>
> While lying on your back, draw your knees to your chest. Place your palms on your knees. Let your knees fall to your sides, to your edge: the place where you feel a stretch that you can breathe into, but not cause injury. Breathe into the stretch. How much can you soften in your pelvis? Allow, especially, the genital muscles to stretch and release. Bring the knees back together when you feel complete. Lower the soles of the feet to the floor. Slide the feet out and rest in savasana.

## Integration Is Very Important

Resting between strenuous poses is critical in creating a healthy balance of energy in your body. Too much *vinyasa* (flow), *bandha* locks and pranayama can create an imbalance, especially in those who are already energized and vital. I can't emphasize enough how important it is to ground the energy. This can be very challenging for young, energized people. Our culture does not support us in slowing down. Many feel like they are on a treadmill and unable to stop. Work becomes the primary focus; if we're not working, then we should be sleeping. So many suffer from anxiety and insomnia as a result. Take the time to slow down your practice. Give time to integrate a series of poses by resting in savasana and child's pose for a significant time, especially after a strenuous flow. This is where the healing happens, when you stop and allow the *prana* to flow throughout the body.

Lighter: Living Tantra

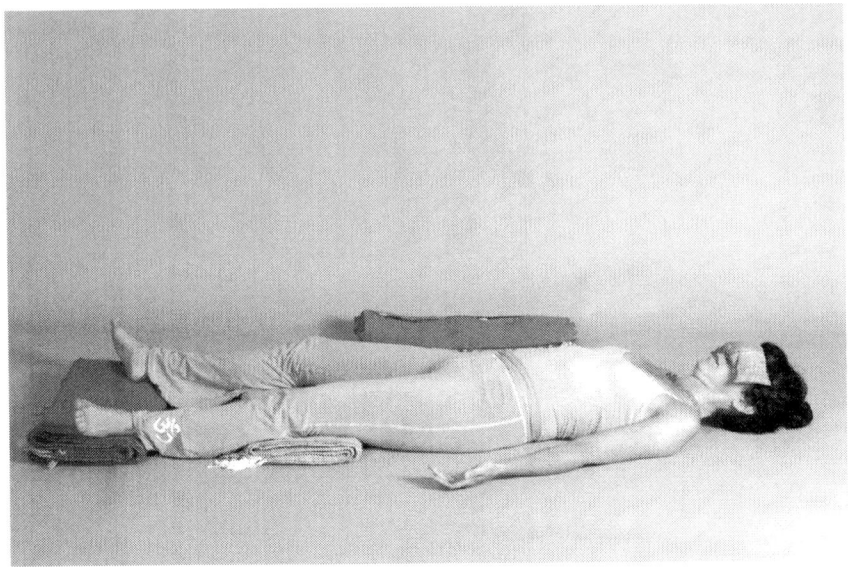

"Savasana"

---

**Six Circles of the Dragon (QiGong)**

My Qigong teacher, Ann Carroll, intuited that this form would be beneficial to me now in my own life. It also turned out that it is an excellent series of movements for strengthening the core. Dominique Ferraro presents Six Circles of the Dragon in her book *Qigong for Women* (2000).

"As she herself pointed out, these movements energetically nourish the three cavities (lungs, stomach and womb), as well as the entire endocrine system. As such, they are excellent for nourishing the core, sometimes called "the heavenly heart of the middle house" because it is located centrally between the upper and lower realms in the body. It is the spirit of the receptive, creative Earth energy residing as the celestial pivot point between the upper yang spirits of light and formlessness, and the deeper yin spirits of darkness and manifesting form.

The Heavenly Pivot is an acupuncture point (also known as Stomach 25) and is located two inches or so to either side of the navel. Its name indicates its position and its ability to move dynamically in multiple serpentine circles emanating from the umbilical central axis. Adjacent and behind Stomach 25 are the kidney points, Ki16, which also are rotated and pivotally energized by the dragon-like circles. These play a key role in cultivating the primordial qi, which is the essential pre-natal or primal life energy we bring with us into this life, and which is foundational for our physical health, for healing and for our overall wellbeing." (Ann Carroll)

Practice the Six Circles of the Dragon every other day to strengthen the heavenly pivot, to maintain a balanced energy body.

Begin each circle with knees slightly bent, legs together.

Breathing for each circle: inhale arms to one side. Exhale arms to the other side.

Repeat each circle six times.

Begin and end each circle (except Circle 5) with palms together at the heart center.

"Movement One for Each Circle"

After completing each circle with your hands at your heart center, close each series of six circles by pointing your palms downward, then place one palm on top of the other just below your navel. Men, place the left palm down first and place right palm on top of left palm. Women do the opposite: right palm down first, then left palm on top.

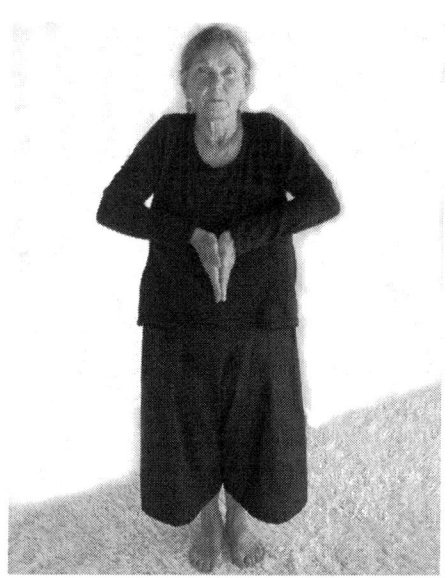

"Closing Movement One for Each Circle"

"Closing Movement Two for Each Circle"

**Contraindications:** Circles 2, 3 and 6 are not advised for anyone experiencing chronic back injuries or has damaged discs. This flow also may be challenging for anyone who is still healing knee injuries.

Circle 1: Place your palms together at the center of your chest. Knees are together. Move your palms to the right, while moving your knees to the left. Bring the palms overhead. Straighten knees. Bring palms to the left, and knees to the right. End with knees at center and palms at center of chest.

Circle 2: Begin with your palms at the center of your chest. Bring your palms to the right. Move knees in opposite direction. Engage your core, by pulling your navel to your spine. Hinge at the hips. Bring your knees to center. Bring palms to feet (or as close as you can get). Stand up, moving palms to left and knees to right. End with palms at center of chest and knees centered.

Circle 3: Begin with palms at center of chest. Bring palms to right. Knees to left. Engage your core, by pulling your navel to your spine. Hinge at hips. Center knees. Extend palms forward, then to the left. Knees to right. End with palms at center of chest standing upright with knees centered.

Circle 4: Place right palm on top of left palm at the center of your torso. Bring left elbow back alongside your torso. Knees go to the right. Bring palms forward and back to center and center knees.

Circle 5: Place left palm on top of right palm at center of your torso. Bring right elbow to the right side of your torso. Knees go to the right. Bring palms forward and back to center. Center knees.

Circle 6: Place palms together at the center of your chest. Bring palms straight overhead. Drop shoulders down and away from your ears. Engage your core, by pulling your navel to your spine. Hinge at your hips. Extend arms forward and bring palms to feet (or as close as you can get). Come up to standing and bring palms back to center of chest.

"Circle One Movement Two"

"Circle One Movement Three"

"Circle One Movement Four"

"Circle Two Movement Two"

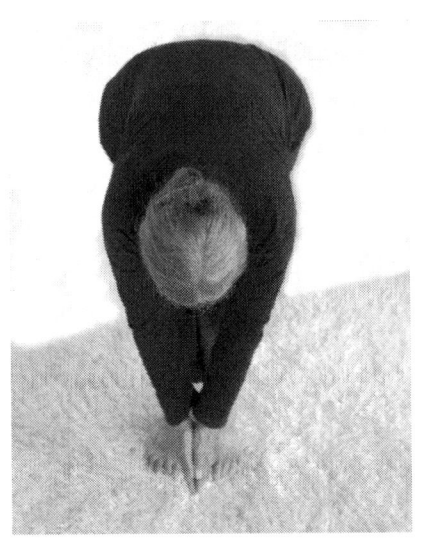
"Circle Two Movement Three"

"Circle Two Movement Four"

Maintaining Your Center and Integrating

"Circle Three Movement Two"

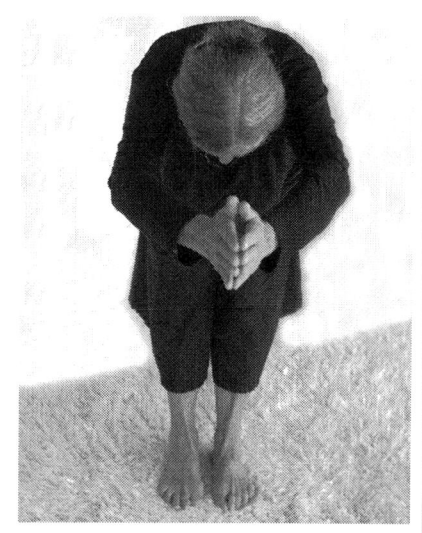
"Circle Three Movement Three"

"Circle Three Movement Four"

"Circle Four and Five Movement One"

"Circle Four and Five Movement Two."

# Maintaining Your Center and Integrating

"Circle Six Movement Two"

"Circle Six Movement Three"

### Qigong Lying Down Meditation

Yang Yang, Ph.D., suggests that we practice the Qigong Lying Down Meditation daily to recharge and restore qi. It is a great way to close a more active Qigong or yoga practice. It can also be done in the morning before you get up for the day or just before you go to sleep. I learned this practice from Dr. Yang when he came to Portland, Maine.

Dr. Yang is known as a master practitioner and teacher within the traditional Taiji and Qigong community, and as a researcher interested in applying the highest standards of Western science to explore and promote Eastern wellness programs. He speaks to medical professionals and practitioners of Qigong and Tai Chi (Taiji) worldwide about the medical benefits of Qigong. He says that by doing this practice daily, we will feel stronger. If you feel depleted, this practice will help. The lying-down exercises are part of his Evidence-Based Qigong and Evidence-Based Taiji programs, and more about the purpose of the lying-down Qigong exercises is detailed in his book *Taijiquan: The Art of Nurturing, The Science of Power.*

1. Lie on the floor or in your bed. Let your knees and feet roll to the sides, with feet about 8-12 inches apart. Arms are along the side the body about six inches from your torso. Palms are up, just like in savasana.

2. Begin by bringing your awareness to your heels and invite them to sink into the floor.

## Maintaining Your Center and Integrating

3. Bring your awareness to your ankles and invite them to sink into the floor.

4. Continue this all the way up the body and down the arms, inviting one body part at a time to sink. If your mind drifts, bring your awareness back to where you left off.

5. When your whole body is more relaxed, envision a ball of energy in your middle *dan tien*, the area just below your navel. (Location of the middle *dan tien* varies depending on the tradition studied.) This ball can appear as a glowing ball of white light.

6. Now, imagine that energy moving down your left leg, up the left side of your body and down your left arm.

7. Do the same on the right side of the body.

8. Now, bring your awareness back to the energy ball at your middle *dan tien* and imagine the energy moving down your left leg, up your right side and down your right arm.

9. Do the same on the other diagonal.

10. Breathe and allow this energy to radiate throughout your body. If you can't feel it, imagine it. Notice how you feel.

11. When you feel integrated and ready, roll to your right side and pause here. When you are ready, place your palms on the floor and push up to sitting.

Close your practice with the Gold Ball Meditation described below.

As an aside, but very relevant, after Dr. Yang's talk, I asked him what to do when one feels they are merging too much with others. He paused a moment and replied, "Do your practice regularly and you won't have that problem." In my experience, he is correct; wise words from a lifelong practitioner of energy medicine.

### Gold Ball Meditation (Taoist)

This Taoist meditation exercise is very grounding. It is a yin meditation that runs yin/Earth/feminine energy up and down the spine to help balance yang/Sky/masculine energy. This exercise brings Earth energy into the energy body.

Come into a comfortable seated position. Feel your sits bones touching the cushion below you. Feel the back of your legs touching the cushion and floor. Inhale and lengthen your spine. Imagine a string is pulling the top of your head toward the sky. Exhale and reach your tailbone toward the Earth, while maintaining that length in your spine. Imagine your tailbone is a taproot reaching into the Earth, all the way to the center, connecting with the heart of the Earth. Keep your chin parallel to the floor. Continue to breathe easily and naturally.

Now imagine a gold ball about the size of a grapefruit in the Earth below you. On an inhalation, guide the gold ball through your pelvis,

## Maintaining Your Center and Integrating

torso and just above your head. Imagine it is moving through a central energy channel along your spine. In yoga we call this the central channel or *shushumna*. Exhale the ball down through your central channel. Repeat.

If you are feeling very anxious or ungrounded, you can imagine the gold ball opening when it is above your head. Then imagine that a warm, thick, gold liquid is pouring down your spine, into the Earth.

Start by doing this practice for five minutes daily and add more time each time you sit. It has been found that it takes about 20 minutes to relax deeply, so aim for 20 minutes each day.

### Gold Ball Meditation

CHAPTER EIGHT

# Sharing Energy

## The Solo Practice is Where the Heart Is

So far in this book I have shared Shiva and Shakti practices that raise or ground energy. These practices will help you to expand into your true purpose. I believe this is the best way to come into connection with others, feeling whole. I highly recommend a dedicated solo practice both before and while sharing energy with another person.

It is during solo practice that one can feel the full spectrum of the transformational and healing benefits of movement, sound and meditation practices.

When yoga became popular in the Western world, I recall discussions with people from India who, over and over again, shared that yoga was done as a solo practice in the home and was very private.

Today, in my practice, I realize why. It is because when taking the time to be alone and come into union with body, mind and spirit — the spirit of oneness — we can have a one-on-one relationship with God (or Goddess, Spirit, the Universe, Higher Power, Inner Wisdom). In this state of oneness, it is possible to experience all that is divine surrounding us, and within us.

Create time for your solo practice. Designate an area in your home that is kept clean, clear and free of distractions. Fill it with decor that inspires and relaxes you. Decide on a regular time that fits into your schedule. First thing in the morning tends to be the best time, before you get pulled into other projects. Your body, mind and spirit will love the routine.

For ideas for your solo practice, take regular classes and study with a master teacher of your choice. You can also use DVDs and podcasts to get ideas. Lie in savasana, close your eyes, breathe and do the poses, movements, meditations or chants that come to your mind's eye.

## Coming Into Connection with Another

When practicing Tantra, one's energy field becomes lighter. This lightness results in a heightening of sensation. Come to a Tantra practice partner grounded, clean and clear. From your highest place, I invite you to choose a partner (which may be the partner you are already with) by using clear and loving communication. You will most likely feel drawn to someone who might be open to such practices. Ask that person if they are interested in exploring Tantra with you and discuss how you each see that unfolding. Will you simply practice together or are you exploring something deeper? In either case, be clear about how you would like your practice sessions to unfold. Would you like to create sacred space? Where will this be? What do you consider to be sacred space? Describe the room. Will there be music or no music? Candles? Scents? Surprises? Discuss your preferences, if you have any, and also what you would prefer not to have present. For example, will your time include discussions about work? Will it include laughter, massage (share what body parts need attention beforehand so you can be present), intercourse or not, a check-in, talk of money, talk about children, trust, breathing, eye gazing, chanting, etc.?

## Eye Gazing

Eye gazing is a simple practice that deepens intimacy and connection. It can be done with anyone you come in contact with, simply by giving eye contact. It can also be done in a deeper way with your practice partner. It is the gateway to the soul.

Come together sitting in front of one another knees to knees (cross-legged). Prop pillows under your bottom and sit on the edge of your pillows. You can also sit in chairs if this helps to align your spine (helpful if your hamstrings are tight). Lower your knees until they are lower than your hips. Inhale and lengthen your spine. Imagine a string pulling the top of your head toward the Sky. Exhale and lengthen your tailbone toward the Earth. Imagine your tailbone reaching to the heart of the Earth. Feel your sits bones on your pillow. As Elysabeth Williamson of Principle-Based Partner Yoga suggests, imagine your pelvis is like an upside down teacup, slightly suctioning the Earth's surface.

With internal awareness, begin to notice your breath. Take a few falling-out breaths. Inhale through the nose and exhale out the mouth with the mouth slightly open and the jaw soft. Let the exhale fall out with a sound, a low tone or a sigh. With each exhale, release thoughts of the past or any future plans. With each inhale, become more present in this moment for your partner practice.

Once centered, begin to raise your eyes and notice your partner sitting across from you. Soften your gaze so 50% of your awareness is on yourself and 50% of your awareness is on your partner. Always feel your connection to yourself and the Earth. If you feel you are moving too far out of your center, close your eyes and re-center yourself.

Some say the eyes are the gateway to the soul. Science now shows that the eyes do connect to neural pathways that hold memories of the past. You may see indications of past memories in your partner's eyes. Hold your partner in compassion as you see where they have come from.

Now, I invite you to notice your partner in this moment. Who they are now?

Finally, notice their fullest potential. Who they are becoming as they transform?

## Synchronized Breathing

Sitting across from your partner, follow the above instructions for eye gazing. When you are ready, begin to notice your partner's breath. You may notice their shoulders rise and fall. Exhaling audibly can help your partner to synchronize with your breathing. Everyone has different lung capacities, so the one with a larger lung capacity may need to hold their breath slightly to let their partner catch up. For both partners, see how much you can slow your breath down and lengthen your breath, while synchronizing with each other. You can also use your hands to show your partner how you are breathing by raising your hand from the pelvis to the throat with your inhale, and then lowering it from the throat to the pelvis as you exhale.

If you get out of synch, laugh, smile and begin again or try it another time. It is best to keep these exercises light and try not to coach or teach each other. Be patient and allow yourselves to synchronize in time.

Synchronized Breathing

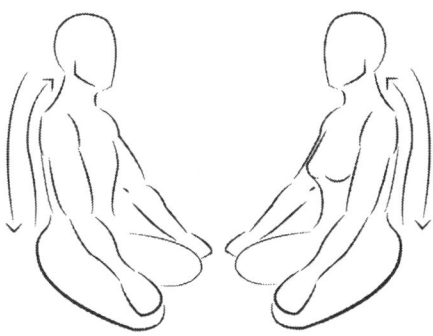

## Circular Breathing

Follow the instructions above for eye gazing and synchronized breathing. Once you are breathing in synch, the person choosing to be in a "masculine" role can hold their breath while their partner exhales. As the person in the "feminine" role begins to inhale energy up from the Earth, the partner holding their breath can begin to exhale energy from the Sky into her pelvis. To clarify, the partner in the masculine role is exhaling from the Sky into his partner's pelvis and the person in the feminine role is inhaling from the Earth and exhaling out her own head into the Sky, and then into his head. You can use your hands to show the motion of your breath as done above in synchronized breathing, but this time the one partner's hands move up, while the other partner's hands move down, to create a circle of energy.

To help to clarify these breathing instructions, the person in the masculine role is exhaling from the Sky out his penis into his partner's vagina. The person in the feminine role is inhaling from the Earth and her partner's penis. This visual usually helps our students to understand this flow of breath and energy. If you are a female/female couple, follow the instructions above or imagine one of you is in the "masculine" role and wearing a "strap on"…or if you would like you can put one on.

This practice can be a bit more complicated for some, so again, if it doesn't flow with ease, laugh, smile and try again. You may want to release it for the time being and try again another time, so there is no pressure to learn it right away.

Sharing Energy

Once you have learned this practice, you can try breathing in and out of each other's heart center rather than head, sending love to each other.

A more advanced practice would be for the person in the female role to sit on the lap of the person in the masculine role, as in the traditional Tantra partner pose called *yab yum*. Begin with eye gazing, then synchronized breathing, then circular breathing. Once you feel you are doing circular breathing, you can add pelvis tilts and thrusts. As you inhale, arch your back, beginning at the pelvis and working up to the heart center. As you exhale, round the back from the back of the heart down to the pelvis, completing by thrusting the pelvis. This movement can activate kundalini energy because of the spine and pelvic movement and because of its erotic nature.

All these practices can be shared in daily life.

Circular Breathing

## Eye Contact

When you greet your partner, your neighbor or your coworker, notice if you are looking directly into their eyes. If not, can you breathe into your next greeting and do so? Notice if you feel a different level of connection after eye contact.

## Hugging a Loved One or Friend

When you greet someone whom you normally hug, notice how long you hug and if you breathe. Can you lengthen your hug a moment or two longer and take a breath?

In our Tantra retreats, we invite students to come to class early to share a "Tantra hug," where we eye-gaze, ask if the person we are greeting wants a hug, then stand together or hug and take three synchronized breaths. This is a practice we did when I was in the Standing Wave community every time we came in contact with another member of the community. I love the tradition so much that I have adopted it for our Tantra to Love™ retreats. It slows life way down and increases intimacy and connection.

In daily life, three breaths can feel like a long time. I invite you to share at least one synchronized breath with each other as you embrace. Take more breaths with willing partners.

## During Lovemaking

Experiment with synchronized breathing during your favorite lovemaking poses. Once you have that technique mastered, begin to add circular breathing. Make it playful. Laugh if it falls apart, rather than blaming or coaching. If a power dynamic ensues, tantric practices are not taking place. Tantra requires a balance of energy. If a practice of sharing breath and energy falls apart, you can start over or let it go until next time. Just don't let it go completely. Stick with it. The rewards are rich. We have yet to teach a student who could not learn circular breathing. Sometimes it just takes a patient and supportive partner.

In order to experience kundalini energy during lovemaking, similar to the solo practice, a regular partner practice is helpful. For example, try adding some Tantra practice gradually to your lovemaking. If you make love a few times per week, let at least one of those times be a tantric practice. If you are enjoying it, add more Tantra sessions to your lovemaking. Blend the two as you choose. Decide what serves both of you by sharing your needs before you connect intimately.

In my case, by age 40, I was tired of the sex I had been having since I was a teenager. I was ready to have a more sacred and energy-based sexual connection. In order to make the shift from our old ways of having sex to a tantric sexual connection, my husband and I chose to be celibate for three months. We practiced only Tantra for those three months and did not have intercourse. It was what allowed us to live a truly tantric lifestyle inside and outside of the bedroom. We had been together about five years at that time. Now, some young people are beginning their sexual relationships by practicing Tantra. No old habits to break.

## When Energy Bodies Merge

When practicing Tantra, as described earlier in this chapter, our energy bodies become lighter. Whether you are connecting with someone who is practicing Tantra or not, if you are not well grounded as a Tantra practitioner, you can easily merge with another person. Merging can present itself in your daily life in different ways. You may notice that you are being unusually empathetic about others' problems. You may actually feel another's pain, think about their problems and even obsess over them as if they were your own to solve. You may feel overly sensitive and even cry easily when watching emotional movies, or at sentimental events. Even if you think you are well grounded, you may sometimes have these experiences, which is a sign that you need to ground even more. Look at merging as a gentle reminder to do your solo practice and Self-care. It's something we are not used to in many developing cultures, where we are instead encouraged to be on the go in order to survive.

During lovemaking, it can be blissful and transformative to merge energy. It is also very important to intentionally and physically take back your energy at the end of a lovemaking session. Come back into yourself fully, so you do not get lost in your partner. This could result in putting your partner's priorities before your own. That doesn't always end well. Tantra asks us to find a balance of giving and receiving. When we do receive, we reap its benefits in the form of increased energy, clairvoyance, deeper connection and the personal power to live our destiny.

One way to take back your energy is to close your eyes and notice your breath. You can also physically move apart and do something that nourishes you, like taking a walk in nature or taking a bath by yourself. Before pulling apart from your partner, honor your time together by bowing to one another in gratitude. You can even say "thank you" and offer a compliment, then lovingly communicate your need for alone time. Those receiving this message can recognize that this request is not a criticism, but a personal need their partner is expressing. It is best not to take it personally, but to take the opportunity to come into your own breath and solo space.

## Grounding Exercises

Grounding exercises should be done daily as maintenance for your newly light and expanded energy body. This is a new way of being in the world. I think you will agree that you will feel more energy and clarity. With these gifts, you will be more capable of living out your destiny in a successful and sustainable way. For this reason, it is worthwhile to find a balance point of being light *and* grounded.

Everyone needs to feel grounded to different degrees. Being grounded often begins with a supportive childhood. Those who did not have one may need to do even more grounding exercises until they have cultivated a Self-love that is no longer dependent on their childhood experience.

Also, those with lighter constitutions, often tall and thin, tend to need more grounding than those who are naturally a heavier build. In Ayurveda, a system of traditional medicine native to India and a form of alternative medicine, those needing more grounding have a *vata dosha* (a Sky-dominant constitution), while those who need less often have a *kapha dosha* (Earth-dominant constitution). Ayurveda states that a balance of three elemental substances (*dosha*) is health, and imbalance is disease. There are three *dosha*: *vata*, *pitta* and *kapha*, though I am only discussing the first two in relation to Tantra.

Similarly, in Traditional Chinese Medicine, the dominant element for a lighter constitution is Wood (spring), while those who are more grounded in nature have more Earth element (winter). In both the Ayurvedic and traditional Chinese systems, we are born with this dominant constitution and it is our destiny to learn to live in harmony and come into balance. Those who are very Earthy, or *kapha*, love Tantra because it lightens them up when they may be overly lethargic. Those who are *vata* in the *Ayurvedic* system or Wood in the Chinese system often need to do more grounding practices when raising energy. I have a *vata dosha* and Wood is my dominant element, while my husband Rene has a *kapha dosha* and Earth is his dominant element. As life partners, we naturally bring balance to each other's lives.

## Ways to ground as a daily practice and as needed:

- Walk in nature.
- Take a bath with salt crystals, in the sea or a natural spring.
- Practice Qigong. (The animal frolic called Bear Walk is particularly grounding. See photo and instructions below.)
- Practice the Gold Ball Meditation (see previous chapter, page 72).
- Eat grounding foods (e.g., roots, nuts, olives, avocados, etc.).
- If your body is craving fat, eat fat. Do not let your old desire to look thin override your body's need for fat to weigh you down. As you practice Tantra, your third eye will expand and your body will begin to choose the foods it needs. Take the time to tune in and listen to what your body really needs, not what the media is telling you is "desirable." A little Buddha belly or what is affectionately know here in Maine as a "Big Maine Butt" will keep you grounded and connected to Self as you expand and connect with others.
- Lie on your Biomat (a heating pad filled with Amethyst crystals. See Resources page for information on this product).
- Practice the pranayama techniques called Alternate Nostril Breathing (see photo and instructions below) and/or Three Part Yogic Breathing (see instructions and photo in Chapter Two).

---

**Bear Walk**

Bear Walk is a Qigong walking meditation that can be very grounding; walking in general can be very grounding. I begin my daily practice with this walk.

1. Come to *santi* stance with right foot about 1 1/2 feet ahead of left foot. Back foot is at a 30-degree angle and front foot is at a

3-degree angle, both feet pointed in the same direction. Knees are bent deeply. Be aware of the kidney point between the ball of the big toe and the pad of the other toes, known as the "Bubbling Well." Spread base of feet to make a connection between the kidney point and the floor or Earth.

2. Bend knees deeply and place palms on back thigh. Torso is twisted toward this thigh.

3. Inhale. Shift weight forward, face forward and bring palms to waist height, facing the ground. Elbows are bent. Come to upright position with knees still bent deeply. Exhale.

4. Bring back foot forward and come back to *santi* stance and repeat above instructions.

Bear Walk Movement One

Bear Walk Movement Two

> **Alternate Nostril Breathing (Standing Wave version)**
>
> 1. This is an easy pranayama practice that can be done anytime and anywhere to help to bring your energy down. This pranayama exercise balances the sympathetic and parasympathetic nervous systems, regulating the fight or flight response one experiences when under stress.
>
> 2. Sit, lie down or stand with a straight spine.
>
> 3. Using your right hand, bring your first and second fingers to the pad of your thumb.
>
> 4. Place your ring finger over your left nostril.
>
> 5. Place the palm of your left hand under your right elbow and brace your arms on your torso. You can also rest your right arm on your chest.
>
> 6. Take a long, full, slow inhale into your right nostril.
>
> 7. Hold your breath as you release your ring finger from your left nostril and place you thumb on your right nostril.
>
> 8. Release the breath by exhaling completely out your left nostril until there is no more air in your lungs.
>
> 9. Now, inhale through the left nostril. Cover the left nostril and exhale out the right nostril.

Sharing Energy

10. Continue alternating inhaling into one nostril and exhaling out the other.

11. Repeat a complete breath (one inhale and one exhale) three, six or nine times. Nine times will promote the most relaxation. Continue longer if needed.

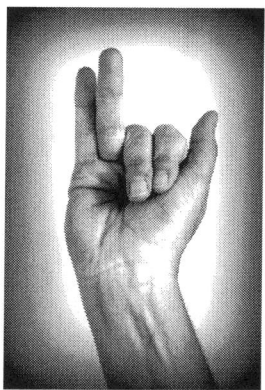

"Alternate Nostril Breathing Hand Position"

"Alternate Nostril Breathing Movement One"

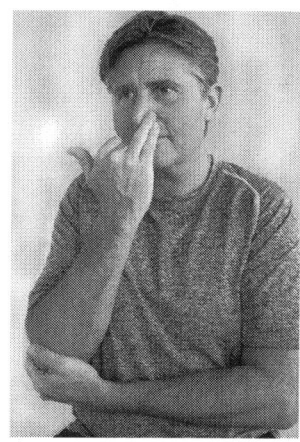

"Alternate Nostril Breathing Movement Two"

CHAPTER NINE

# Some Final Thoughts

In summary, I suggest one begins a Tantra and Qigong practice by studying Tantra practices with master teachers. You can also get started by using my yoga podcasts available for free on our website www.tantratolove.com, as well as the Qigong practices available on our YouTube channel www.youtube.com/PranaHeals. When your energy centers begin to open, seek counsel from those master Tantra and Qigong teachers who can support you effectively. If you are not finding that your teachers are able to support you, then seek professional counsel to address the emotions that stir as your body, mind and spirit adjust to a new way of being. Welcome transformation by keeping your ego in check and being aware of your shadow. Study and practice conscious communication to clearly, honestly and lovingly communicate the changes you are experiencing and the new way you are choosing to live and be. If you choose, once you have established a regular solo practice, begin to explore sacred sexuality practices with a partner, using the conscious communication skills you have developed. When practicing sacred sexuality, always remain deeply connected to yourself. The grounding and lifestyle practices shared throughout the book will help you to remain centered and balanced as you embark on a Tantra lifestyle. If kundalini imbalances occur, deepen your grounding practices. Enjoy the journey back to your True Self. I am available to support you through private sessions, workshops, retreats and our Tantra to Love™ Lifestyle Mastery Program. I can effectively guide and assist you from around the world via phone and Skype. Namaste. Jai Ma!

*"May we all shine our light upon others and heal, one authentic, truly joyful smile at a time."* ~Prana Regina Barrett

# Appendix

**Divine Love Meditation**

*This practice is more advanced. For an introduction to tantric meditation and grounding yourself, I recommend beginning first with the Gold Ball Meditation, then the Third Eye Meditation. Practice these ongoing, before practicing the Divine Love Meditation. Practice the Divine Love Meditation when you feel ready and as needed.*

This meditation was channeled while I was experiencing an extreme migraine due to heightened kundalini energy rising. I received a vision of an Indian man pouring water over my head, possibly from a past life, as I appeared to be Indian as well.

First, envision water being poured over your head. This water is soothing, softening and cleansing. Imagine it cleansing all the allergens, toxins and tensions from your body.

Soften the top of your head (your crown chakra). Inhale divine love from the Sky through your crown chakra and through your shushumna (central channel), all the way to the heart of the Earth. (The inhale is technically being drawn in from the nose.)

Exhale and allow the breath slowly to rise up your front body and out your mouth. Allow your exhalation to wash over your heart and throat, softening anything holding in those chakras.

When practiced regularly, notice if your communication transforms to a more loving form. Also, notice how this style of communication affects your relationships with others.

## Divine Love Meditation

# Glossary of Sanskrit and Chinese Terms

*Ananda* means bliss.

*Asana* is one of the eight limbs of yoga philosophy. A movement practice that release contractions within the body. By applying alignment principles, *prana* or life force can flow through energy channels (*nadis*) to other parts of the body for optimal health. The intention behind asana practice is to allow the tantra practitioner to sit in meditation for long periods of time.

*Bandhas* are "body locks," or ways of contracting three areas of the body during *asana* or pranayama practice. Bandhas seal oxygen and energy (*prana*/life force) in the body while holding the bandha(s) for a certain number of breaths. When the breath and bandha(s) are released, prana radiates throughout the body from the center of the bandha.

*Chakras* are energy centers located throughout the body. The main chakras are located along the spine and in the hands and feet. Energy channels called *nadis* connect chakras to organs throughout the body.

*Dan tien* is an energy center in Traditional Chinese Medicine and a focal point for Qigong exercises.

*Deity* is a mythological being, who may be thought of as holy, divine, or sacred. Some religions have one supreme deity, others have multiple deities of various ranks.

*Dosha* is an Ayurvedic constitution that one has from birth. Ayurvedic practitioners can help you balance your doshas with foods, spices, oils and other natural remedies.

*Jalandhara bandha* is a yoga breathing technique that locks energy in the body by drawing the chin to the chest.

*Kapha* is an Ayurvedic constitution that is Earth-energy dominant. People who are kapha-dominant tend to be slower moving, larger, content and easy going, and have more moisture in their hair and skin.

*Kashmir Shaivism* is an ancient hindu tantra tradition practiced by householders. Its premise is that of Universal Consciousness in that we are all part of the whole. Shiva is considered God, the entirety of the Universe, and the identification with Shiva will lead to unwavering bliss-consciousness.

*Kriya* is a yoga practice that assists in awakening kundalini energy. Kriyas are also yoga practices that are meant to create a certain result. Kriya is also a term used to describe the movements that result from awakened kundalini energy.

*Kundalini* is the energy that lies dormant at the base of the spine. When activated, it moves up the spine and interacts with the chakras, the energy centers along the spine.

*Mantra* is a chant that vibrates the energy centers and channels within the body. When mantras are repeated regularly, they can change thought patterns.

*Mula bhanda* is a yoga breathing technique, also known as pranayama, which locks energy in the body by squeezing the muscles between the anus and genitals and pulling that muscle upward into the center of the body. This muscle is also known as the perineum.

*Pranayama* is a yoga breathing technique.

*Purusha* is located at the second chakra, just below the navel. This is thought to be where our pure essence lies: the true identity, the Self.

*Qi* (sometimes spelled chi) is a term from Traditional Chinese Medicine for the life force energy of all living things.

*Qigong* is a practice of aligning breath, movement and awareness for exercise, healing and meditation. With roots in Traditional Chinese Medicine, martial arts and Taoist philosophy, Qigong is traditionally viewed as a practice to cultivate and balance qi (chi) or life energy. From a philosophical perspective, Qigong is believed to help develop human potential, allow access to higher realms of awareness, and awaken one's "true nature."

*Sangha* is spiritual community, where members practice together and raise the vibration to a higher level.

*Savasana* is a yoga pose also called "corpse pose." When in savasana, one is practicing the art of dying in order to be reborn. It is a very restorative pose that is done to integrate a more active yoga practice.

*Seva* is selfless service: volunteering without any expectations of receiving anything in return. Seva is thought to burn or clear karma.

*Shakti* is the divine feminine energy, which originates from the Earth. She is also a Hindu goddess whose is referred to as The Divine Mother.

*Shiva* is the divine masculine energy, which originates from the Sky. It is also the name of one of the main Hindu deities, who transforms the ego.

*Shushumna* is the central energy channel that surrounds the spine.

*Uddiyana bandha* is a yoga breathing technique that locks energy in the body by pulling the abs up from the public bone to the diaphragm.

*Ujai* breathing is pranayama, where the practitioner constricts the throat and inhales and exhales through the nose. It should be audible, like the sound of fogging a mirror.

*Vata* is an Ayurvedic constitution that is described as very Sky-energy dominant. People who have vata constitutions tend not to like cold, dryness or wind. They are often thinner, have quicker impulses and dryer hair and skin.

*Vinyasa* a yoga style that involves changing a pose for each breath, making it flowing or always moving. This style developed from *Ashtanga* yoga, which is an older form of yoga that includes both static poses and flow.

*Yab Yum* is a traditional tantric partner meditation position where the person in the "feminine" role sits on the lap of the person in the "masculine" role. Each partner places one palm on their partner's sacrum (the boney plate at the base of spine) and the other palm on the back of their heart. Both partners should adjust with props, so their spines are straight. This pose can be done in a chair or on the edge of your bed.

*Yin* is a term from Traditional Chinese Medicine for feminine, soft energy.

# Citations

Ballentine, Rudolph, M.D. *Kali Rising: Foundational Principles of Tantra for a Transforming Planet.* Tantrikster Press, 2010.

Ferrraro, Dominique. *Qigong for Women. Healing Arts Press*, 2000.

Jung, C. G. *Psychology and Religion: West and East.* (2nd ed.) Princeton: Princeton University Press, 1975.

Lind-Kyle, Pat. *Heal Your Mind, Rewire Your Brain.* Energy Psychology Press. 2010

Snowden, Ruth. *Teach Yourself Freud.* New York: McGraw-Hill, 2006. pp. 105–107.

Zweig, Connie. *Meeting the Shadow.* Los Angeles: J.P. Tarcher, 1991. p. 24.

# Recommended Resources

Amethyst Richway Biomat: follow Biomat link at www.tantratolove.com

Free download of ho-oponopono prayer: http://www.thereisaway.org/Ho'oponopono_cleaning_meditation.htm

Yoga Flow Podcasts: free at www.tantratolove.com

Qigong movements: free at www.youtube.com/PranaHeals

*The Art of Sexual Ecstasy* by Margot Anand, 1989, Penguin Putman Inc., New York, NY

*The Breath of Tantric Love* DVD by The Ecstatic Living Institute www.ecstaticliving.com

*The Seven Chakras Poster* by Integrative Yoga Therapy www.iytyogatherapy.com

David Deida is a well-known Tantra educator who explains the masculine and feminine aspects of Tantra as it relates to psychology. www.deida.info/

*Healing Sex: A Mind Body Approach To Healing* by Staci Haines, Cleis Press, San Francisco, CA

*Ipsalu Formula: A Method for Tantra Bliss* by Bodhi Avinasha, 2003 info@ipsalutantra.com

*Jewel in the Lotus: The Tantric Path to Higher Consciousness,* Third Edition by Suntaya Saraswati and Bhodi Avinasha, 1995, Ipsalu Publishing info@ipsalutantra.com

*Kali Rising* by Rudolph Ballentine is a powerful philosophy about the masculine and feminine aspects of Tantra and our cultural evolution. www.kalirisingthebook.com

*Osho Tantra: The Supreme Understanding,* Fifth Edition 2003, Tao Publishing, Pune, India

*Osho Transformation Tarot* cards, St. Martin's Press, New York, NY

*Patanjali's Yoga Sutras*; Swami Satchidinanda's version or Alistair Shearer's translation

*Taijiquan: The Art of Nurturing, The Science of Power* by Yang, Yang, Ph.D., Zhenwu Publications, 2005

*Tantra: The Art of Conscious Loving* by Charles and Caroline Muir, 1989, Mercury House, San Francisco, CA

*Tantra Secrets for Men* by Kerry Riley, 2002, Destiny Books, Rochester, VT

## Recommended Resources

*Urban Tantra* by Barbara Carellas www.urbantantra.org

*The Way of Qigong: The Art and Science of Chinese Energy Healing* by Kenneth Cohen www.kennethcohen.com

*Women's Anatomy of Arousal* by Sheri Winston, 2010, Mango Garden Press, Kingston, NY www.intimateartscenter.com

# About the Author

Prana (Regina Barrett), BS, MIA, ERYT, CYT is the founder, lead Tantra educator and yoga therapist at Tantra to Love™. Prana founded the *Tantra to Love™ Lifestyle Mastery Program and 60 hour Educator Certification.* She has created the audio pod casts *Self Love: Gentle and Restorative Asana Flows with Photos of Poses.* Prana shares a Tantra yoga, shamanic and Qigong path, while creating a safe container for physical and emotional transformation.

Prana has spent the past 17 years embodying a tantric lifestyle in community. Her teachings have been informed by in-depth studies of Osho, Ipsalu, Standing Wave, Kashmir Shaivism, Kundalini Yoga, Qigong and Phoenix Rising Yoga Therapy. She currently resides in Portland, Maine, where she shares a Tantra and Taoist lifestyle with her husband, John Rene Berard.

Made in the USA
Charleston, SC
18 March 2014